THE CRIME BUFF'S GUIDE TO OUTLAW PENNSYLVANIA

RON FRANSCELL
AND
KAREN B. VALENTINE

Guilford, Connecticut

All photos by Karen B. Valentine unless otherwise noted.
Test design: Sheryl Kober
Layout: Sue Murray
Project editor: Lauren Szalkiewicz
Maps by Alena Joy Pearce © Morris Book Publishing, LLC

Library of Congress Cataloging-in-Publication Data

Franscell, Ron, 1957-
 The crime buff's guide to outlaw Pennsylvania / Ron Franscell, Karen
B. Valentine. — First Edition.
    pages cm. — (Crime buff's guides)
 Summary: "The Crime Buff's Guide to Outlaw Pennsylvania is the
ultimate guidebook to the crime, injustice, and seedy history of the
Keystone State. With photographs, maps, directions, and sites to visit,
this collection of outlaw tales serves as both a travel guide and an
entertaining and informational read. It is a one-of-a-kind exploration
into well-known and more obsure sites in Pennsylvania that retain
memories of bandits and their scandalous deeds"— Provided by publisher.
 ISBN 978-0-7627-8833-0 (pbk.)
 1. Outlaws—Pennsylvania—History. 2. Crime—Pennsylvania—History.
I. Valentine, Karen B. II. Title.
 HV6452.P39F73 2013
 364.109748—dc23
                                                              2013018900

Printed in the United States of America
10 9 8 7 6 5 4 3 2

CONTENTS

To my father, Martin Schneider, a constant inspiration
And to my son, Aaron Valentine, my partner in crime
—Karen

Crime takes but a moment, but justice an eternity.

—ANONYMOUS

INTRODUCTION:
HISTORY ENTANGLED

Pennsylvania is an old soul, settled by Europeans in the 1600s and by Native Americans long before that. In 1791, when Los Angeles was a dusty Spanish pueblo (population 139), Philadelphia was the capital of the United States and the fledgling nation's largest city, boasting nearly forty thousand people.

And, where there are people, there is crime. For every Daniel Boone, Margaret Mead, and Robert Fulton born in Pennsylvania, there was an Alfred Packer, Darlie Routier, and George Hennard.

This book expanded both of our worlds. Karen gained new appreciation for her home state, and lifelong westerner Ron dove into a deeper past. Pennsylvania's history, good and bad, has shaped America. From the congested streets in the City of Brotherly Love, to a lonely field near Shanksville, what has happened in Pennsylvania has changed, moved, and sometimes shocked us.

This is a trip to Pennsylvania's darker side, where seemingly idyllic places reveal secrets—the stone wall where a kidnapped child was last seen; the park where the first school-shooting in America happened; the birthplaces of outlaws who came to infamy in other states; and the graves of the innocent and the guilty.

Let this book be your window to our past. Appreciation of history begins in the places where it happened. And through the magic of the Global Positioning System (GPS) you can stand in precise historic spots, as close as modern technology and imagination can put you. We've made every attempt to put you literally within inches of this past.

This is certainly no ordinary guidebook. You won't find many suggestions for places to sleep or eat, although you might often find such spots by chasing these ghosts. Rather, consider this a history book that tells you exactly where to stand to get fleeting glimpses of the past and present—and maybe a bit of the future.

Pennsylvania is so full of history that you can hardly walk a block without stepping over it. So slow down and take some time to find it. History is how we know, how we learn. And being there makes all the difference.

—Ron Franscell & Karen B. Valentine

HOW TO USE THIS BOOK

The entries in this book are divided into four chapters, encompassing one thematic chapter about the infamous Molly Maguires and three geographic chapters (Eastern Pennsylvania, Philadelphia Metro Area, and Western Pennsylvania, including the Pittsburgh Metro Area). Each entry has physical and GPS directions that will let you stand in the footsteps of history—not in the general vicinity, but literally on a spot relevant to one of Pennsylvania's most notable and infamous crimes or figures.

Crimes big and small have been committed every single day since mankind began to distinguish right from wrong. This book cannot begin to aggregate every injustice, every crime, every inhumanity ever visited upon Pennsylvania, although even the smallest crime certainly affects victims, survivors, and communities as much as the most celebrated crimes in our history. And in some cases here, we have chosen only a few representative sites. So please don't be offended if you feel we've overlooked a crime or site you believe should have been included.

A word of warning: Many of these sites are on private property. Always seek permission before venturing onto private land. Don't trespass. It's not only rude, it's illegal. And, as you will see, there's already enough crime in Pennsylvania.

We made every effort to be precise in our facts and directions, but, being human, we might have erred. If you believe we should include a certain crime in future editions—or if you see an error that should be corrected—please send a note to Ron Franscell/OUTLAW PENNSYLVANIA, c/o Globe Pequot Press, 246 Goose Lane, PO Box 480, Guilford, CT 06437; or email *editorial@globepequot.com.*

A NOTE ABOUT GPS ACCURACY

GPS readings are affected by many things, including satellite positions, noise in the radio signal, weather, natural barriers to the signal, and variations between devices. Noise—static, interference, your car roof, or competing frequencies—can cause errors up to 30 feet. Clouds, bad weather, mountains, or buildings can also skew readings up to 100 feet.

While we've tried to make every GPS coordinate in *The Crime Buff's Guide to Outlaw Pennsylvania* as precise as possible, we can't be sure you'll visit under the same conditions. The best possible way to get an accurate reading is to be sure the satellites and your receiver have a clear view of each other, with no clouds, trees, or other interference. If your device doesn't bring you to the right spot, look around. It's likely within a few paces.

1

EASTERN PENNSYLVANIA

THE MAN WHO WOULDN'T DIE
Allentown

The former Toto home is at 2420 Walnut Street, or GPS 40.59081, -75.50695. This is private property.

Back in the early 1980s, Tony and Frances Toto owned a pizzeria together, but after suffering through seventeen years of Tony's flagrant womanizing and physical abuse, Frances decided to kill him.

First, she laced his soup with rat poison. But Tony only got queasy and cured himself with a few doses of a common, pink digestive aid.

Then she rigged a trip-wire across the steep stairs outside their house. He stepped on it, and it broke.

Then Frances hired a hit man to brain him with a baseball bat. But, as Tony walked past his would-be assassin, who was hiding behind some bushes, the assailant's bat got tangled in the foliage, and Tony strolled on, oblivious.

Then the frustrated wife persuaded a friend to rig Tony's car to explode when he turned the key. But the jerry-rigged device fizzled, and Tony drove off unexploded.

Then Frances hired her daughter's boyfriend, Anthony Bruno, to shoot Tony in the head as he slept. Although the bullet lodged in his brain, Tony still didn't die. Frances "nursed" him back to health by putting an overdose of sleeping pills in his soup. Instead of killing him, the drugs probably saved his life by slowing his metabolism, allowing the wound to heal.

Then Frances hired two delinquent teenage cousins to shoot Tony in the heart with his own gun while he lay in bed. But the dullard cousins weren't exactly sure where his heart was, so they just

Eastern Pennsylvania

NEW YORK

Oakland

South Canaan

Milford

Loyalsock Township

Wilkes–Barre
Larksville

Stroudsburg

Hanover Township
Catasauqua
Allentown
Lower Macungie Township

Bath
Easton
Bethlehem
Salisbury Township
Coopersburg

Pottsville

Reading
Schwenksville
Denver
Phoenixville

Pennsburg
New Hope
Wrightstown
Collegeville

Harrisburg
Reinholds
Lititz
Manheim Township
Lancaster
Carlisle

Nickel Mines
North Hopewell Township

Coatesville
Malvern
Newtown Square
Philadelphia

Pennsbury Township

MARYLAND

DE

NEW JERSEY

N

0   2   4 Miles

shot Tony in the chest, managing to avoid every major organ. Tony even sat up and asked what the noise was.

That night, the cousins bragged to their friends about being hired as hit men. On a tip, police went to the Totos' house and found Tony wounded.

Frances confessed everything . . . and Tony bailed her out of jail, hired her a lawyer, and even testified on her behalf. When asked how he could forgive her, he replied, "Everyone makes mistakes." He pledged to wait for her until she served her time, saying, "We've got a lot of good years ahead of us."

In 1984, Frances was convicted but served only four years in prison, after which she was released into Tony's open arms. At last report, they were still married.

The 1990 film, *I Love You to Death*, starring Kevin Kline and Tracey Ullman, was based on this wacky case.

CULLEN'S KILLING GROUNDS
Allentown, Bethlehem, and Easton

St. Luke's Hospital is at 801 Ostrum Street in Bethlehem, or GPS 40.60897, -75.39258.

Charles Cullen was an Angel of Death—a registered nurse who murdered patients he was supposed to heal. He cut a deadly swath across two states, killing up to forty people in seven hospitals and one nursing home over a period of sixteen years before he was caught in 2003. Despite his spotty work history and lingering suspicions of wrongdoing, nobody ever raised a red flag.

Because of a nursing shortage and Cullen's willingness to work odd hours in the most stressful departments, no one in authority checked his background too closely. If they had, they would've discovered twenty suicide attempts, two psychiatric admissions, an arrest for stalking a co-worker, missing medications, and an inordinate amount of patient deaths while he was on duty.

Cullen typically injected patients with an overdose of drugs like digoxin, insulin, and norepinephrine. Although most of his killings happened in New Jersey, he was responsible for at least eleven in Pennsylvania—seven at St. Luke's, two at Lehigh Valley Hospital (I-78 and Cedar Crest Boulevard in Allentown, GPS 40.56712, -75.52397), and one each at Liberty Nursing Home and Rehabilitation Center (535 North 17th Street in Allentown, GPS 40.60448, -75.49587) and Easton Hospital (250 South 21st Street in Easton, GPS 40.68678, -75.24282). During his Pennsylvania period of mayhem, Cullen lived at 831 Fernwood Street in Bethlehem, or GPS 40.62587, -75.36325.

The facilities later claimed they feared a lawsuit from Cullen if they'd given him bad references, but their inaction opened them up to millions of dollars in lawsuits from the relatives of his victims. Because of Cullen, new laws were passed in Pennsylvania and New Jersey that would hold medical facilities blameless for disclosing an employee's bad work record.

Between the two states, Cullen was sentenced to eighteen life terms.

THE D-DAY BANK ROBBERY
Bath
The former First National Bank is west of the intersection of Route 329 and Airport Road, at GPS 40.70362, -75.42172.

On June 6, 1986, Martin Appel and Stanley Hertzog burst into the First National Bank of Bath and started shooting, without asking anyone to give them any money. Two tellers—Janice Confer and Hazel Evans—were killed instantly. Secretary Jane Hartman ducked under her desk but was seen by Appel, who shot her dead. Office manager Marcia Hauser and customer Thomas Marchetto were wounded but survived. The robbers got a mere $2,280 for their bloody rampage.

The bank janitor got their license-plate number, and police soon arrested the robbers. In Appel's trailer, they found the guns used by the robbers and the stolen cash in the refrigerator. The two were convicted. Hertzog received a life sentence, and Appel was sentenced to death. Appel, freely admitting the crimes, asked to be executed right away without appeals. The judge complied.

But Governor Robert Casey, a death-penalty opponent, refused to sign the death warrant throughout his eight years in office. When the next governor, Tom Ridge, signed the death warrant, Appel immediately appealed. In prison, he'd received thyroid surgery and now claimed his defective thyroid had made him delusional, causing his death-wish. The new appeal process took fifteen years, until Appel and prosecutors agreed on a plea deal for three life terms.

The bank was closed and later re-opened as a Sovereign Bank, but it too is now closed. The empty building sits up on a ridge, abandoned and forlorn.

BABES IN THE WOODS
Carlisle

Westminster Memorial Gardens is at 1159 Newville Road. To get to the gravesite, go in the middle entrance of the cemetery and straight down to a large marker on a traffic island between Sections C and G, or GPS 40.20390, -77.22381.

On November 24, 1934, the bodies of three little girls, huddled together, were found in the forest twenty feet off Route 233 North, two miles north of Pine Grove Furnace State Park, near Centerville. A historical marker is at the site at GPS 40.06587, -77.30507. A pathologist determined they had gone eighteen hours without food and had been strangled or suffocated.

Within a day, ten thousand people came to the Ewing Funeral Home in Carlisle to view the bodies, but no one recognized them. The story became an instant sensation, and offers came in from the

Historical marker at the site of the discovery of the "Babes in the Woods"

public nationwide to pay for a decent burial for the children. They were all politely declined, and the local American Legion raised the money for a funeral.

On the same day the girls were found, the bodies of a man and woman were discovered near Altoona, an apparent murder-suicide. The dead couple was Elmo Noakes and his lover, Winifred Pierce, who had driven from California seeking jobs. They'd brought along Noakes's two young daughters, Dewilla and Cordelia, and his step-daughter, Norma Sedgwick.

Police theorized that Noakes killed the girls to spare them from starvation. He and Pierce then drove as far as their old junker would take them before it broke down in Altoona. With their last few dollars, they bought a rifle to kill themselves.

The family was reunited in death at Westminster Memorial Gardens in Carlisle. Noakes and Pierce are in unmarked graves in Section E, about 100 feet from the girls.

A WOMAN SCORNED
Catasauqua

The former Katrinak house is at 740 Front Street, or GPS 40.65559, -75.47794. This is private property.

When Patricia Rorrer called for the umpteenth time to speak to her ex-boyfriend, Andrew Katrinak, his current wife, Joann, reached her limit. She told Rorrer in no uncertain terms that Andrew was now happily married to her, they had a little baby, and she was never to call again. In North Carolina, where she was then living, Rorrer seethed as Joann hung up on her. She got into her car and began driving north.

A short time later, on December 15, 1994, Joann called her mother-in-law to reconfirm their shopping date with four-month-old Alex. Unknown to her, Rorrer had broken into the basement and was listening to the conversation. When it was over, the ex-girlfriend cut the telephone wires and confronted Joann at gunpoint as she was settling Alex into his car seat.

Rorrer forced Joann to drive to a remote rural area near where Rorrer had once stabled her horse. In the woods, Rorrer ordered Joann to her knees and shot her once in the head, then smashed her skull with nineteen vicious blows. She left the baby alone beside the corpse to die, returned the car to the house, and went back to North Carolina.

When the bodies were found, Andrew fingered his jealous ex-girlfriend as the likeliest suspect, partly because he knew she was familiar with the remote site of the killings. Eventually, Rorrer was convicted and sentenced to two life terms.

Joann and Alex are buried together at Saints Cyril and Methodius Roman Catholic Cemetery, Williams Street, just south of Crest

Park Court, South Bethlehem. Their common plot, with a beauti-fully engraved headstone, is on the right side, halfway down the hill from the cemetery entrance, at GPS 40.60435, -75.34863.

THE LAST DAYS OF THE GENTLEMAN BANDIT
Coatesville

The former Cammie house is at 2 Spruce Street, or GPS 39.970241, -75.854657. This is private property.

Despite the fact that he never got rich robbing trains, Bill Carlisle (1890–1964) was one of the most popular—and longest lived—bandits of the Old West.

Born Walter Cottrell to an aging Civil War veteran and his young wife, toddler Walter aka "Bill" was sent to an orphanage in York, Pennsylvania, after his mother died. At fifteen, he joined a circus, and soon moved to Denver. In 1915, he bought a little glass gun that he planned to fill with candy as a Christmas gift for his niece, but it proved to be an infamous career move.

After wrecking a train, he reportedly held up passengers with his candy-filled glass pistol. After another robbery, he sent a telegram to the Union Pacific, thanking them for the loot. In the 1940s—after getting out of prison—he toured as a promoter for Hollywood westerns. Once, he even stopped at the Union Pacific Museum in Omaha to confirm that a gun they displayed was, indeed, the one he used in the hold-up.

Going straight and becoming an honest citizen proved easier for Carlisle than robbing trains. He married Lillian Berquist in 1937, worked a few jobs, and then owned a popular campground in Laramie, Wyoming, where he ran a little cafe. His customers were often travelers who just wanted to meet the last of the Wild West's train bandits.

In 1946, he wrote a book, *Bill Carlisle: Lone Bandit*, illustrated by famous artist Charles M. Russell. Today, only 177 original copies are known to exist.

Carlisle once told his young great-nephew that his favorite TV western was *Gunsmoke*, because it came closest to representing the authentic Old West.

When his wife died in 1962, Carlisle moved in with his beloved niece, Hilda Cammie of Coatesville. In 1964, at age seventy-four, he died of cancer at her home. For fifty years, Carlisle's final resting place was unknown because a surviving sister was embarrassed by her bandit-brother's past and buried him in a secret grave, creating a half-century mystery.

But using interviews and never-before-seen family records, we found him for this book: He was buried under his legally-assumed name, Will Carlisle, beside his father at Riverview Cemetery, 3300 North Main Street in Wilmington, Delaware. His grave, marked simply "WBC," is in Section C, Lot 139, or GPS 39.759115, -75.530604.

For more about Carlisle, see *The Crime Buff's Guide to the Outlaw Rockies*.

ANN RULE'S CHILDHOOD HOME
Coatesville

The former Stackhouse home is at 922 West Chester Road, or GPS 39.98174, -75.80509. This is private property.

The reigning queen of true-crime writing, Ann Rule has over thirty best-selling books, all of them still in print. But the former Ann Stackhouse has Pennsylvania roots: She graduated from Coatesville High School, Class of 1949, and her yearbook shows she was quite an achiever. She still is, producing a new book about every nine months.

In 1971–72, she worked at a late-night suicide hotline alongside a personable young man named Ted Bundy. When their shift was over, Bundy graciously walked Rule to her car and warned her to be careful, because he didn't want anything bad to happen to her. They maintained a friendship even after they both quit the hotline.

Rule's ordinary freelance-writing career was launched into a new orbit in 1974, when she got a contract to write a book about an unknown killer who was abducting and murdering beautiful young women around Seattle, where she lived. Soon Rule discovered, to her horror, that Ted Bundy was that murderer.

Her book about Bundy, *The Stranger Beside Me*, was an immediate smash, and she became a staple on TV and the lecture circuit. The Justice Department called on her to help develop the Violent Criminal Apprehension Program (ViCAP), the nationwide program to coordinate information on active serial killers.

Ann Rule still lives in the Pacific Northwest.

THE LYNCHING OF ZACHARIAH WALKER
Coatesville

Hephzibah Baptist Church Cemetery is at 2237 Strasburg Road. Victim T. Edgar Rice's grave is in Section 4, east of the church and near the top, or GPS 39.95218, -75.80940.

Zachariah Walker was one of hundreds of black laborers recruited from the South to work in the Worth Steel Mill in Coatesville. But although they were now in the allegedly tolerant North, he and the others soon realized they were regarded with the same disdain by an entrenched white citizenry and were segregated to dilapidated shacks on the edge of town. Unable to participate in the town's acceptable activities, Walker and his brethren spent most of their off-time drinking in the local bars. On August 12, 1911, this pastime would prove fatal.

Stumbling home drunk after a day-long binge, Walker spotted some white millworkers on the road near the mill. Pulling out his handgun, he fired over their heads, intending just to scare them. Nobody was hurt, but the shots attracted the attention of the mill's security guard, T. Edgar Rice. He and Walker scuffled, and Walker shot the guard dead. Too unsteady to make it home, Walker crawled into the hay loft of a nearby farm and fell asleep.

Rice's body was soon discovered, and a posse set out to find Walker.

The next morning Walker awoke to the sounds of his pursuers and fled into the woods. Climbing a tree, he watched the posse pass beneath him and finally decided to kill himself rather than be caught. He shot himself in the jaw and dropped wounded to the ground below.

After his arrest, he admitted he'd killed Rice, but in self-defense. He was taken to Coatesville Hospital, where he was bandaged and chained to a cot. Only one policeman guarded him.

Into the night, two thousand angry townspeople gathered in the streets and talked of a lynching. Fired up, several masked men burst into the hospital and overpowered the cop and nurses. Finding Walker chained to the cot, they dragged him and his bed down the street to a neighboring farm to the cheers of the following throng. Along the way Walker pleaded for mercy, but there would be none.

At the farm a large pile of wood was set on fire. Walker (still chained to his cot) was thrown into it. Screaming in agony, Walker tried to crawl out, but several men pushed him back in with rakes. Twice more, Walker emerged from the flames only to be forced back into them. The crowd watched calmly as his horrific death-cries finally faded away. When the fire cooled, onlookers picked the place clean, gathering pieces of Walker's body, clothing, and bones as souvenirs, along with the chains, charred wood, and even blades of grass. What was left of him fit into a shoe box.

Fifteen men and teenagers were tried for the lynching but all were acquitted.

When a historical marker about the lynching was dedicated in 2006, the people of Coatesville had mixed emotions about it. Some felt that it would help race relations, while others thought it was honoring a murderer. In any event, it stands today on Doe Run Road (Route 82), southwest of Coatesville at GPS 39.97099, -75.83183.

THE MANDERACH MURDERS
Collegeville

The former Your Kidz and Mine children's clothing shop is now a phone store at the Collegeville Shopping Center, South 2nd Avenue, near Charles Street, at GPS 40.18330, -75.45203.

When Lisa Manderach entered the kid's store with her toddler daughter, Devon, on September 10, 1995, manager Caleb Fairley was astounded. For the game of "Dungeons and Dragons," Fairley had created a love-object that resembled the beautiful, dark-haired Lisa. With the mother and daughter alone in the store, he locked the door and made a move on Lisa. She fought him furiously but was no match for the beefy twenty-two-year-old. Enraged by her rejection, Fairley strangled the mother and daughter to death.

Lisa's body was dumped at an abandoned health club, and Devon was thrown down an embankment inside Valley Forge National Park. Today, a cross marks the spot where Devon was found on South Inner Line Drive, along a sharp turn with a brown sign, VALLEY CREEK BELOW at GPS 40.08856, -75.45475.

Fairley was sentenced to life in prison.

Mother and child are buried at St. Patrick's Roman Catholic Church Cemetery, 2400 DeKalb Pike, Norristown. The grave is marked by a double heart-shaped headstone at GPS 40.13542, -75.31826.

MURDER IN THE CHURCH
Coopersburg

Trinity Evangelical Lutheran Church is at 2170 Route 212, or GPS 40.52926, -75.29554.

Plump and frumpy Mary Jane Fonder had a crush on Pastor Gregory Shreaves, who didn't share her ardor.

Even so, Fonder burned with jealousy at the kindness and financial support Shreaves and his congregation showed to fellow parishioner, perky and attractive Rhonda Smith. The last straw was when Smith got up at a church service and thanked everyone for helping her. In fourteen years Fonder had never received a dime from the congregation, although she had been through some very hard times. Worse, the clique of women who ran the social gatherings never included her in their plans. It wasn't fair, and something had to be done about it.

A temporary church secretary, Smith was sitting alone in her office on January 23, 2008, when someone shot her twice in the head. Smith died later after being disconnected from life support.

The murder weapon was found at a nearby lake and traced back to Fonder. And in Fonder's day-planner for January 23, she had written, "Rhonda Murdered." Directly under that was the word "Hairdresser," an appointment she had dutifully kept after shooting her rival.

After Fonder's conviction and life sentence, police took a new look at the strange disappearance of her father, eighty-year-old Ed Fonder, who hadn't been seen alive since 1993. Fonder had complained to friends about caring for the cantankerous old man after her mother's death. She claimed that he had gone out for a newspaper while she slept and never returned, although she continued to cash his Social Security checks. No charges have ever been brought in that case.

Smith is buried at Hellertown Union Cemetery, 85 Main Street in Hellertown. Her grave is on the left side of the cemetery, toward the back and close to the road, at GPS 40.57243, -75.33578.

LUNA'S DEATH DRIVE
Denver

Sensenig and Weaver Well-Drilling Company is at 1439 Dry Tavern Road, or GPS 40.21088, -76.05685. A large wooden cross stands next to the creek where the body was found at GPS 40.21097, -76.05736.

Jonathan Luna seemed to be living the American dream. Rising from the mean housing projects of the South Bronx to become an Assistant US Attorney in Baltimore, he was married to a doctor and had two beautiful children. But on December 4, 2003, the dream ended in a nightmare. When he left his job at 11:30 p.m. and drove off into the night, he entered a mystery as weird as *The Twilight Zone*.

Instead of going home he drove to Delaware and stopped at an ATM to withdraw $200 from his bank account. He then crossed into Pennsylvania and got onto the westbound Pennsylvania Turnpike, exiting at the Reading-Lancaster Interchange. When he paid his toll ticket, the clerk saw a spot of blood on it but nothing else suspicious as Luna pulled away.

By 5:30 a.m. company workers spotted a car with its front-end planted in the small creek nearby and investigated. Blood streaked the driver's window, and Luna's body was in the water. An autopsy revealed he'd been stabbed thirty-six times with his own pen-knife but died from drowning.

No reason for his journey could ever be determined, and no arrests have been made.

THE MISSINGEST MAN IN AMERICA
Easton
Judge Crater's childhood home is at 631 Ferry Street, or GPS 40.68944, -75.21550.

In the Roaring Twenties, corrupt New York Supreme Court Judge Joseph Force Crater (1889–1930) was a worthy cog in Tammany Hall's crooked political machine and reportedly received a fortune in kickbacks and graft.

On August 6, 1930, he met some friends at a steakhouse in Manhattan. After dinner he bid them goodbye at the curb and got into a taxi, which drove him down 45th Street and into oblivion. The forty-one-year-old judge was never seen again. He soon became a running joke, with announcements like, "Judge Crater, call your office," on the radio and in movies.

Judge Crater's childhood home

In 2005 ninety-one-year-old Stella Ferrucci-Good died, leaving a note saying that her late husband Robert Good, along with New York policeman Charles Burns and Burns's cabbie brother Frank, had murdered Crater and buried him under the boardwalk on Coney Island at the present-day site of the New York Aquarium. If so, he may literally be "sleeping with the fishes."

GIRLS GONE WILD
Easton

The former Hetzel/Bloss home is at 120 West Saint Joseph Street, or GPS 40.68244, -75.20921. This is private property.

In 2000, a volatile mix of teenage angst and a lesbian love triangle led to the brutal murder of Devon Guzman.

Devon was a free-spirited girl who couldn't seem to commit fully to either Michelle Hetzel or Keary Renner, the two other teenagers who competed for her affection. Although married to Brandon Bloss, Michelle wanted Devon. On Michelle's dime they'd traveled together to St. Croix for a week in tropical luxury, even exchanging vows and rings in their own private "marriage ceremony."

But back home old troubles resumed. Michelle was still living with Brandon, and Devon was living with Keary at the Mineral Springs Hotel, Apartment #3, 4306 North Delaware Drive, just north of Easton (GPS 40.75322, -75.19695). A jealous Keary often confronted Devon about her frequent, not-so-secret meetings with Michelle, often ending in shouting, broken furniture, and a few cuts and bruises. The night of June 14, 2000, was one of those nights.

Michelle and Devon had argued earlier, ending with Devon throwing Michelle's "wedding ring" in her face. Keary accosted Devon as soon as she came in the door, and another brawl ensued. When it ended, Devon stormed out, heading toward Michelle's house.

But an hour later nobody seemed to know where Devon was. For several hours Keary and Michelle searched for her, eventually arriving at Hugh Moore Park (now Delaware Canal State Park), Route 611 South at GPS 40.68792, -75.20499. Devon often went to the scenic spot to meditate.

Sure enough, Devon's car was there. But when Keary and Michelle looked in, they saw Devon's lifeless body on the back seat. Devon was in a fetal position with a knife in her hand and a hypodermic needle nearby, but when investigators lifted her from the car, more horrific injuries became apparent. This was no suicide.

Her throat had been cut nearly to her spine, and her face and arms were covered in bruises.

After cops spotted a severe human bite mark on Brandon's lower arm—a bite later matched to Devon's teeth—Michelle and Brandon were charged with Devon's murder. Each accused the other in the slaying, but both were convicted and sentenced to life in prison.

Devon was buried at Northampton Memorial Shrine, 3051 Green Pond Road, Palmer Township. She's in Section J, Grave 122, or GPS 40.69065, -75.26578.

THE CHEW CLUE
Easton

Easton Cemetery is at 401 North 7th Street. Go through the main entrance and turn right, following the road through the cemetery until it ends at a small metal fence. Stop there and walk down the curving walkway behind it to the large receiving-vault at the bottom at GPS 40.69569, -75.21639.

Richezza Williams was a troubled thirteen-year-old runaway from New York when she started selling drugs for some violent Easton traffickers.

On July 28, 1996, Williams was visiting her friend Kathleen Sagusti at 719 Bushkill Street (GPS 40.69381, -75.21933), when three members of the gang—Corey Maeweather, Stanley Obas, and Kwame Henry—burst through the door and accused Williams of ripping them off. They beat her, and then dragged her into the basement, where they tortured the screaming girl for an hour with red-hot coat hangers, a corkscrew, and an electrical cord, pouring bleach into her wounds. When the screaming stopped Sagusti watched from the window as the men carried a large cardboard box down the back alley. Checking the basement she discovered Williams was gone.

Fearing for her own safety, Sagusti kept her mouth shut. But a week later Henry and Maeweather roughed her up, too. Sagusti called the police and reported the attacks on herself and Williams. Investigators soon discovered the dead Williams in the nearby cemetery vault—and on the floor beside her body, they found a large wad of red chewing gum, bearing a distinct tooth impression.

Police records reflected that when Maeweather was arrested for Sagusti's assault, he was chewing Big Red gum and had several more sticks in his pockets. When a forensic odontologist compared the crime-scene gum-wad with Maeweather's teeth, he declared them a match. In order to avoid the death penalty, Maeweather confessed, claiming a rap song had driven him to do the torture/murder. Unimpressed, the judge sentenced him to life in prison. While listening to the judge, he was still chewing a wad of Big Red.

In 1998, Henry was arrested on the island nation of Trinidad and also sentenced to life. Obas remains at large.

ROBERT DURST GOES SHOPLIFTING
Hanover Township (Lehigh County)
Wegman's Supermarket is at 5000 Wegman's Drive, or GPS 40.66584, -75.38882.

Pennsylvania is a magnet for crazy millionaires, and Robert Durst definitely qualifies. The scion of a vast real-estate fortune that includes several skyscrapers in Manhattan, Durst failed at the family business and at his marriage to the former Kathleen McCormack. When Kathie disappeared from their summer cottage after returning from a party on January 31, 1982, her friends were convinced Durst had killed her. But, without a body, the police were stymied.

Eight years later, on Christmas Eve, 2000, Robert's best friend, Susan Berman, was murdered in her Los Angeles home after she told reporters that she was writing a book that would "blow the lid off of things." She was referring to an exposé of the Las Vegas mafia, but some, including Durst, thought she was talking about

Kathleen's disappearance. Once again, the police had no evidence, and Durst was never charged.

Durst went underground. Wearing women's clothes and a wig, he pretended to be Dorothy Ciner, a deaf-mute living in a derelict apartment in Galveston, Texas. His neighbor across the hall was crusty curmudgeon Morris Black.

In late September 2001, Morris also disappeared. That is, until his headless torso and other body parts were found floating in Galveston Bay. A newspaper in one of the trash bags containing the body parts had an address sticker that led cops to the apartment house where Durst and Black lived. Both their apartments were bathed in blood. More evidence at the scene pointed to Durst, who was arrested a week later. He paid his $300,000 bail and fled the jurisdiction to Pennsylvania.

He didn't stay hidden long. On November 30, 2001, a guard at Wegman's grocery store watched a security camera as a bald man with shaved eyebrows plucked a single bandage from a box on the shelf and placed it under his nose. The thief then walked toward the door, pocketing a chicken-salad sandwich on his way out.

Outside, the guard confronted the shoplifter and called police. The thief was Robert Durst, who had $500 in his pocket and another $38,000 in his car as he stole about $8 worth of stuff.

Durst was sent back to Texas, where he claimed he killed seventy-one-year-old Black in self-defense and was eventually acquitted of murder. He then pled guilty to bail-jumping and evidence-tampering (for dismembering his neighbor's body) for which he spent only three years in prison, including the time spent waiting for trial.

Kathie Durst's body has never been found, and nobody has ever been prosecuted for the slaying of Susan Berman. Durst has remarried and received a settlement of $65 million from his family's business.

PENNSYLVANIA'S ELECTRIC CHAIR
Harrisburg

The State Museum of Pennsylvania is at 300 North Street, or GPS 40.26562, -76.88588.

From 1913 to 1962, the electric chair—nicknamed "Old Smokey"—ushered 350 criminals (only two of them women) to their deaths. The last one was Elmo Lee Smith on April 2, 1962, for the brutal rape and murder of sixteen-year-old Mary Ann Mitchell in Lafayette Hill. Her body, badly beaten and covered in symbols written in lipstick, was found dumped in a gully. Smith confessed shortly after his arrest but later recanted, to no avail. After Smith's electrocution the chair was retired and given to the state museum, which has never displayed it.

Pennsylvania executions are rare these days. Only three men have died by lethal injection since the state's executions resumed in 1992. The last of these was arguably the most deserving—Gary Heidnik in 1999. Executions are carried out at the State Correctional Institution at Rockview, 1 Rockview Place in Bellefonte. The death chamber is outside the prison walls in a former field hospital at GPS 40.84973, -77.77600.

See also "Gary Heidnik's House of Horrors" (Philadelphia Metro).

KARMA IS A . . .
Harrisburg

The accident scene was the southbound lane of the 1300 block of Cameron Street, or GPS 40.27416, -76.87783.

On July 27, 1999, a tipsy Pennsylvania State Representative Thomas Druce got behind the wheel of his car after a night out with friends. As he tooled along Cameron Street in his taxpayer-leased Jeep, he didn't see the obstacle ahead of him. Before he could stop he plowed into pedestrian Kenneth Cains and killed him on the spot. Instead of stopping and calling for help, Druce sped away in a panic.

Near the capitol building, he stopped under a streetlight and assessed the damage to his car. A headlight was smashed, and the front bumper was torn loose. Fearing that suspicion would be raised if he had the vehicle fixed in Harrisburg, he took it to a repair shop in his home district of Warrington, near Philadelphia.

He then filed a fraudulent insurance claim, saying he'd hit a construction barrel on the turnpike. After the Jeep was repaired, he exchanged it at the leasing company for a new one, thinking he was home-free. The old Jeep was subsequently sold and shipped to New York.

But tips soon trickled into the Harrisburg Police, fingering Druce for the hit-and-run. He staunchly denied any involvement, although this time he claimed he'd hit a street sign.

Intrigued by the change of story, investigators tracked the Jeep to its new owners and found small quantities of Cains's hair and blood still stubbornly clinging to the vehicle. They then followed the trail to the repair shop and inspected the bumper, which also yielded incontrovertible forensic evidence.

Confronted with these findings, Druce confessed and pleaded guilty—not to vehicular homicide—but to leaving the scene of an accident, tampering with evidence, and filing a false insurance claim. He got four years in prison and was ordered to pay $100,000 in restitution to Cains's family.

Ironically, as a state representative, Druce had voted for a law mandating jail time in any fatal hit-and-run.

THE PAXTON BOYS
Lancaster

The Fulton Opera House is at 12 Prince Street, or GPS 40.03808, -76.30797. The rear wall is all that remains of its time as a colonial workhouse. A memorial plaque at GPS 40.03799, -76.30846 commemorates the tragedy that took place there.

The church and grave of Rev. John Elder, commander of the "Paxton Boys"

In the 1700s, many white settlers in the then-frontier regions of central Pennsylvania hated Indians. They felt the colonial government in Philadelphia was too far away for safety and too lenient on the natives. They were on their own, and the only real law was survival.

So a band of vigilantes formed in the town of Paxton (now part of Harrisburg). Calling themselves the "Paxton Boys," they made it their mission to kill as many Indians as they could find. Their leader, Reverend John Elder, preached fire-and-brimstone sermons against the "heathen savages," stirring the passions of his flock. Known as "The Fighting Parson," he preached with a Bible in one hand and a gun in the other at the Paxton Presbyterian Church, 3500 Sharon Road, Harrisburg (GPS 40.26364, -76.82979). Built in

1740, the church is still being used today. Reverend Elder's grave is in the churchyard cemetery at GPS 40.26349, -76.82983.

Whipped to fevered pitch, the "Boys" would venture into the countryside to hunt down hostile natives who had raided their homesteads. But they weren't picky and killed any Indians they found, hostile or not.

From the time of William Penn, the Conestoga Tribe had lived in peaceful harmony with their white neighbors at Conestoga Indian Town, Safe Harbor Road, and Indian Marker Road, Manor Township, four miles southwest of Millersville, at GPS 39.95987, -76.40031. (A large boulder with a plaque marks the spot today.) Only twenty Conestogas lived in the town, and, on December 14, 1763, thirteen of them were out in the surrounding white villages selling their baskets and wares. A snowstorm stranded them there overnight, leaving only seven others sleeping serenely in their town.

Swooping in without warning, the Paxtons attacked, killing six of them, including two women, a child, and an old man. They then set fire to the village. The lone survivor was a boy named Chrisly, who escaped and ran for help.

When Colonial Governor John Penn got the news, he ordered the remaining thirteen Conestogas to be held safely in Lancaster. The town's authorities grudgingly placed them in the county workhouse.

Incensed by this perceived coddling, the Paxtons banded together in force—up to a hundred strong—and marched toward Lancaster. Despite hearing rumors that the Paxton Boys were again on the warpath, Lancaster officials posted only two guards at the workhouse—the sheriff and the soon-to-be-needed coroner. A British regiment was stationed in town, and could have been pressed into service to patrol the streets, but they were never asked.

Swarming into Lancaster, the Paxtons gathered at the workhouse. The sheriff told them to disperse, but the mob ignored him and broke down the door. The Conestogas fled into the courtyard, but were trapped by the workhouse's high walls. The entire tribe was annihilated, including Chrisly. Angered by the slaughter, Governor Penn ordered the Paxtons arrested, but they never were.

But the Paxtons weren't done. They planned another raid on 140 peaceful Lenni Lenape natives in Bethlehem, all converts to Moravian Christianity. Seeking sanctuary in Philadelphia, the natives were kept on Province Island under British guard.

A delegation sent by Penn—including the indomitable Benjamin Franklin—met the Paxton leaders at a tavern outside Philadelphia in Germantown to diffuse the situation. A crisis was averted.

While the meeting went on, some of the Paxtons amused themselves by taking potshots at the rooster weathervane atop the Reformed Church in Germantown's Market Square. The church has been torn down and replaced, but the weathervane, bullet holes and all, has been preserved at the Germantown Historical Society at the end of the square at 5501 Germantown Avenue (GPS 40.03426, -75.17192).

The workhouse was eventually demolished, and the Fulton Opera House was built on the site in 1852. Before he became an infamous assassin, John Wilkes Booth was a celebrated actor who performed at this theater. It's still in operation and has been designated a national landmark.

A SON'S MURDEROUS GREED
Lancaster
Woodward Hill Cemetery is at 511 South Queen Street. The Hitchcock/Benson mausoleum is in front, to the right of the entrance at GPS 40.02943, -76.30372.

Margaret Benson was heiress to a large tobacco fortune that her ungrateful son Steven couldn't wait to get his hands on. Margaret's father, Henry Hitchcock, founded Lancaster Leaf, the largest tobacco distributor in the country at the time.

Margaret, her daughter Carol, and Carol's illegitimate son, Scott, who was adopted by Margaret, lived at 1515 Ridge Road

(GPS 40.04475, -76.34003). Steven, a screw-up who failed at everything he attempted, lived across the street at 1510 Ridge Road (GPS 40.04475, -76.34039) in a home his mother bought him.

After Margaret's husband died, the Bensons moved to a gated community in Florida, where Steven continued his pattern of making messes for his rich mother to clean up. With his latest business venture failing, and chafing under his mother's control, Steven decided to get his inheritance sooner, rather than later.

On July 9, 1985, he planted a bomb under his mother's SUV and herded his family into the vehicle, pretending they were going to look at some investment property. He made sure to place Scott in the driver's seat and his mother in the front passenger seat, where the bomb would have the biggest impact. Carol got into the back seat.

Steven claimed he forgot something in the house and went inside. Sweltering in the Florida summer heat, Carol opened her door as Scott turned the ignition key—an act that saved her life.

The SUV exploded into a fireball. Margaret and Scott were killed in the blast; Carol was severely burned but survived to tell of Steven's strange actions that morning.

Convicted for the murders, Steven was given a life sentence, which he's now serving. Margaret (1922–1985) and Scott (1963–1985) were brought home to Lancaster for burial. They rest together with the family patriarch at Woodward Hill.

THE STALKING OF LAURIE SHOW
Lancaster

The Oaks Condominiums are at Oakview Avenue and Acorn Boulevard. The Show condo, No. 92 Black Oak Drive, is inside the complex at GPS 40.03373, -76.23908. This is private property.

Lisa Michelle Lambert, nineteen, was a force to be reckoned with.

When she and her boyfriend, Lawrence Yunkin, briefly broke up in the summer of 1991, he began dating sixteen-year-old Laurie Show.

But within days of the break-up, a hysterical Lambert called him, blubbering she was pregnant and demanding that he return to her. She then phoned Show's mother, Hazel, and ordered her to forbid Laurie from seeing Yunkin. It worked: Laurie sent Yunkin back to Lambert.

Everyone thought that settled it . . . everyone but Lambert.

Hell-bent on punishing her rival, Lambert launched a vicious campaign against Laurie. She followed her everywhere, physically attacked her, and called the Show condo almost daily with vicious threats. The Shows went to the police about the harassment, but without anti-stalking laws at the time, they were powerless.

Laurie begged Lambert in vain to leave her alone. Once, Lambert confronted Laurie in a parking lot, punching and shoving her. The Shows filed assault charges against Lambert.

When Lambert learned of the complaint, she was furious. Disguising her voice and pretending to be Laurie's guidance counselor, she called Hazel, asking to meet her at the school at 7 a.m. on December 20, 1991. Hazel went to the school, but the counselor didn't show up.

Suspecting a set-up, Hazel raced home to find her daughter barely alive, lying on the floor in a pool of blood. She had been beaten, her throat was cut, and a rope was tied tightly around her neck.

With her dying breath, Laurie whispered, "Michelle did it."

Police quickly arrested Lambert, Yunkin, and their friend Tabitha Buck. Each blamed the others for the killing. Eventually, all three were convicted of Show's murder after Yunkin turned state's evidence; Lambert and Buck got life and Yunkin got ten to twenty years.

After a series of jailhouse complaints, Lambert got a new trial, but with the same verdict and sentence.

Laurie was buried at Bridgeville Evangelical Church Cemetery, Route 322, just west of Bridgeville Road in Beartown/Narvon. Her grave is on the left side, halfway to the back and along the fence, or GPS 40.11125, -75.99023.

In 1994, Hazel Show succeeded in getting an anti-stalking law passed in Pennsylvania.

MARY JO KOPECHNE'S GRAVE
Larksville

St. Vincent's Cemetery is on Mountain Road just northwest of Warman Street. The grave is in the first section from the entrance, ten rows up the hill at GPS 41.26376, -75.94696.

Once a secretary to US Senator Robert Kennedy, Mary Jo Kopechne (1940–1969) was a twenty-eight-year-old political worker living in Washington, DC. On July 18, 1969, she attended a weekend reunion of RFK campaign workers on Martha's Vineyard. Kopechne left the party before midnight with US Senator Ted Kennedy, who'd offered her a ride to catch the night's last ferry . . . but they never arrived. Kennedy's Buick plunged off a Chappaquiddick bridge into a pond, trapping Kopechne inside the overturned car. Kennedy later

Mary Jo Kopechne's grave

claimed he tried to rescue her but gave up and went to his hotel. He didn't report the accident until the next morning. By then, Kopechne had already been found dead.

Some believe Kennedy had been driving drunk and panicked, or even tried to cover up his involvement, but nothing has ever been proven. He eventually pleaded guilty to leaving the scene of an accident. His driver's license was revoked for a year . . . and his presidential ambitions were permanently dashed.

Ted Kennedy died in 2009 and is buried beside his brothers John and Robert in Arlington National Cemetery (Section S, Site 45-B, or GPS 38.881174, -77.071396).

For more details, see *The Crime Buff's Guide to Outlaw Washington, DC* (Globe Pequot Press, 2012).

FAMILY VALUES
Lititz
The former Borden home is at 15 Royal Drive, or GPS 40.14224, -76.28898. This is private property.

Despite their strict religious upbringing and home schooling, teenagers David Ludwig and Kara Borden were carrying on a torrid sexual relationship behind the backs of their fundamentalist-Christian parents. On November 13, 2005, Kara sneaked home at 5:30 a.m., after spending the night in David's bed, and was caught by her mother as she climbed through the living room window.

Her parents, Michael and Cathryn, peppered her with questions, and as the argument heated up, Kara's cell phone beeped with a text message. Grabbing it out of her hand, Michael looked at the name—David Ludwig. Her parents had already warned her to stay away from the nineteen-year-old, who was way too old for fourteen-year-old Kara. Kara claimed she and David were in love and planned to marry. Angrily disagreeing, her parents ordered Kara to summon David right away for a "discussion."

David came armed with a rifle, a hunting knife, and three pistols. One of the pistols was tucked under his shirt; the other weapons were hidden in a towel on the back porch.

Kara and her sister Katelyn waited in the kitchen as their parents harangued David for more than thirty minutes that his relationship with Kara was both sinful and illegal. The Bordens finished by forbidding him from ever seeing their daughter again. As Michael showed David out, the teen drew the handgun and shot him in the head, killing him. He then shot Cathryn before she could even get out of her chair. She, too, died immediately.

Kara fled at the first shot, and Katelyn locked herself in the bathroom to call 911. Just as David was driving away, Kara came running to his car, jumped inside, and exclaimed, "I'm so thankful to see you." She told him she knew he'd killed her parents, but she wanted only to be with him.

They fled to Indiana, where state troopers arrested them after a high-speed chase. Extradited back to Pennsylvania, the teens were seen as a modern-day Charlie Starkweather and Caril Ann Fugate, a teenage thug and his underage girlfriend who had killed her family then embarked on a killing spree across Nebraska in 1958.

The news media had already discovered that Ludwig's father was a militant survivalist, who had built a bunker on their property at 422A West Orange Street (GPS 40.15363, -76.31918) and stocked his "hobby room" with fifty-two different firearms. Cable news talk shows had a field day with Christian fundamentalism, gun rights, home schooling, and right-wing paranoia.

Eventually, David pleaded guilty to the murders and was sentenced to two life terms. Kara was never charged.

Michael (1955–2005) and Cathryn (1954–2005) were buried at Landis Valley Mennonite Cemetery Annex, left at the intersection of Landis Valley Road and Kissel Hill Road in Manheim Township. The graves are at GPS 40.08994, -76.28268.

ANOTHER TEENAGER RUNS AMOK
Lower Macungie Township

The former Howorth home is at 4524 East Texas Road, or GPS 40.55493, -75.53864. This is private property.

On March 2, 1995, four days after the skinhead Freeman brothers declared open season on parents, another Lehigh Valley youth joined the party.

Jeffrey Howorth seemed to be an average seventeen-year-old—a high school swimmer and a Boy Scout. But he wasn't a great student, and it worried his parents, George and Susan, who expected better. So when Jeffrey failed a Spanish quiz and scored poorly on his SAT, he made sure his parents would never find out.

After school he went home and loaded his father's rifle, then waited for his parents to arrive. George was the first one inside and was greeted by five shots, which killed him instantly.

Fifteen minutes later Susan came home and saw her husband crumpled on the floor. As she looked up at Jeffrey in surprise, he fired into her face. Despite her injury she ran toward the garage, but Jeffrey dragged her back inside, finishing her off with eight more shots.

Fleeing in the family car, Jeffrey got as far as Missouri before he ran out of money and gas.

At Jeffrey's trial his brother Steve told the court how Jeffrey had once threatened to kill him just for suggesting he use mouthwash, and how much his brother admired the "cool" skinheads. He then read aloud a note Jeffrey had written after the killings: "Steve, in case I forgot to do this, I wanted to nail a piece of paper to your forehead that said I told you I would do it. Remember? You can't say I didn't warn you."

The jury acquitted Jeff of murder by reason of insanity, and he was sent to a high-security mental hospital, where he remains to this day. George and Susan were cremated, and their ashes were buried in the Memorial Garden, Panel #4, of Asbury Methodist

Church, 1533 Springhouse Road, Allentown. The gravesite is at GPS 40.61256, -75.54440.

See also "The Skinhead Murders" (Salisbury Township).

IT'S NOT HEART SURGERY
Loyalsock Township
The former home of Miriam Illes is at 2440 Sheridan Street, or GPS 41.25466, -76.95659. This is private property.

In the 1990s, Dr. Richard Illes was chief heart surgeon at Williamsport Hospital, and his wife Miriam worked beside him as his perfusionist. When she decided to quit her job to care for their young son, she picked pretty, young, blond Katie Swoyer as her replacement. Whether she had a lapse of judgment, or was testing her husband's fidelity, no one will ever know.

If it was a test, Richard failed. As Miriam stayed home in their mansion at 138 Lamont Drive, Cogan Station (GPS 41.32192, -77.06085), Richard and Katie had an affair. When Miriam heard about it, she moved out and took their son with her. Knowing his wife could take him to the cleaners in a divorce, the doctor put a plan in motion, insuring Miriam for $250,000.

On January 15, 1999, as Miriam talked on the phone to a friend, she stood perfectly framed in the kitchen window. The friend suddenly heard the crash of breaking glass as Miriam screamed, "Oh my God!" She'd been shot dead through the heart.

Police immediately suspected the doctor, especially after his big insurance pay-out, but they had no hard evidence. Dr. Illes went about his life, moving to Texas, then Spokane.

But police kept digging. In time, they found the murder weapon in a creek bed and the sneakers that had made the footprints behind the house. But the best find of all was a manuscript they dredged up from the doctor's computer. This brilliant man—a heart surgeon—had actually written a book called, *Heartshot: Murder of the Doctor's*

Wife. In it, he detailed every aspect of the crime, from the sniper waiting in the woods behind the house, to Miriam's death by the gunshot through the window, and some details known only to the killer.

When he was extradited back to Pennsylvania in 2002, the doctor tried to explain away the manuscript as a way to make sure the police wouldn't forget about Miriam's slaying. They didn't. Illes was found guilty and sentenced to life in prison without parole, which he is now serving.

MASS GRAVE AT DUFFY'S CUT
Malvern

A historical marker stands on the northwest corner of the intersection at North Sugartown Road and Holly Lane, or GPS 40.033561, -75.529587. The mass grave's actual archaeological dig sites are on nearby private property owned by the railroad.

Early American history was forged by immigrants who came to a new country dreaming of a better life. Unfortunately for some, the dream swiftly faded into bitter reality.

In the summer of 1832, a small band of fifty-seven Irish immigrants took jobs building a railroad line in a spot named Duffy's Cut near Malvern, just west of Philadelphia. But within eight weeks, they were all dead and buried in an unmarked mass grave near the tracks. For decades it was believed they'd died in a cholera outbreak and were buried quickly in the mass grave to avoid a bigger epidemic.

But in 2002, two brothers, William and Frank Watson, came across a secret file left to them by their grandfather, who had worked for the railroad. It hinted at the possibility of darker circumstances.

So the Watsons began an archaeological exploration in the mass grave at Duffy's Cut. Since 2009, they have unearthed seven sets of remains, and with the help of ground-penetrating radar, have found the rest buried thirty feet deep in the nearby woodland.

What they found shocked them: One skull had holes with traces of lead on the edges, suggesting a bullet wound. It also had a gash that appeared to have been inflicted by a hatchet. Other skulls showed signs of blunt force trauma around the time of death.

The Watson brothers—both historians and professors—believe that most of the fifty-seven immigrants likely died of cholera, but some of the unfortunate railroad workers might have been killed by anti-Irish vigilantes, agitated by class and nationalistic passions, and a fear of disease.

The archaeology was shut down in 2011 by Amtrak, which owns the land where the mass grave was found. The railroad claimed the excavation was too close to active rail tracks to be exhumed safely. But talks are continuing to allow the dig to continue in the general area of GPS 40.0367, -75.5337. This is private property, and trespassers have been arrested.

Five of the exhumed remains finally got the proper funeral they never had. They were reburied in an elaborate 2012 ceremony at West Laurel Hill Cemetery, 215 Belmont Avenue, Bala Cynwyd, at GPS 40.014733, -75.223729. The occasion was celebrated with bagpipes and a funeral procession, and the placement of a hand-carved, ten-foot-high Celtic cross grave marker.

A sixth set of remains have been tentatively identified as a man named John Ruddy, and the Smithsonian is hoping to connect him to modern-day relatives via DNA. Ruddy's remains will be returned to Ireland for burial. (The seventh body found by the Watsons has not yet been removed.)

Many of the artifacts unearthed in the Watsons' Duffy's Cut Project are displayed at the Gabriele Library, Immaculata University, 1145 King Road in Immaculata at GPS 40.02977, -75.5704.

NO GOOD REASON
Manheim Township

The Haines's former home is at 85 Peach Lane, or GPS 40.09127, -76.31149. This is private property.

Sixteen-year-old Alec Kreider was a straight-A student who belonged to a small clique of geeks that included his best friend, Kevin Haines. The two were inseparable, spending nearly every day together.

On the night of May 12, 2007, Maggie Haines, just home from college, ran to her neighbor's house and told them something terrible was happening at her home. Police were summoned, and they found Kevin and his parents, Tom and Lisa Haines, stabbed to death in horrific fashion. The case went unsolved for a month.

But after a half-hearted suicide attempt over a lost love, Kreider was put in a mental hospital, where he confessed to his therapist that he had murdered the Haines family. When investigators pressed for reasons, Kreider's best excuse was that Kevin had been annoying him lately by loudly chewing his food at lunchtime.

While awaiting trial in the historic, castle-like Lancaster County Prison, 625 King Street, Lancaster (GPS 40.03964, -76.29229), Kreider showed no sign of remorse, telling another inmate that killing Kevin was "interesting."

Kreider was convicted and received three life sentences.

JFK PARAMOUR SLAIN
Milford

Milford Cemetery is on Route 209, just east of the junction with Route 206. Mary's grave is at GPS 41.31445, -74.80446, next to the large mausoleum of Governor Gifford Pinchot.

Mary Pinchot Meyer (1920–1964) was an enigma. Born into a wealthy, prominent Pennsylvania family of socialists, the path of her privileged life meandered among some of the most famous

Mary Pinchot Meyer's murder inspired conspiracy theories related to her love affair with JFK.

people of her day: Justice Louis Brandeis, Mabel Dodge, Katharine Graham, Timothy Leary, Ben Bradlee and, eventually, a lover named John F. Kennedy.

A Vassar graduate, Mary Pinchot met Marine Lt. Cord Meyer in 1944, and they married a year later. Although Meyer led several left-wing groups after World War II, there's evidence he was also working secretly for the CIA. By 1951, he was officially a CIA employee running Operation Mockingbird, designed to influence American media, and put many reporters on the CIA payroll. Mary, a sometime-journalist, was briefly considered but was ultimately judged to be a risky asset because of her spontaneous love affairs.

In 1954, a new young senator from Massachusetts named John Kennedy and his wife, Jackie, moved into a sprawling estate just down the road from the Meyers' home. Mary and Jackie became quick friends and often walked together. At the same time, Mary's sister Antoinette had married *Newsweek* reporter (and future *Washington Post* editor) Ben Bradlee.

The Meyers divorced in 1958, and Mary began a series of flings, while resuming an abstract-expressionist painting hobby. In late 1961, the single, charming, and notoriously frisky socialite visited her old friend and then-president John Kennedy at the White House. An intimate affair began. She told friends that she and JFK had sex about thirty times and often enjoyed marijuana or LSD that she brought to their trysts.

JFK was assassinated in November 1963. Eleven months later, Mary Pinchot Meyer finished a painting in her studio in Georgetown and took a walk on the C&O Canal's towpath. Two men changing a tire nearby heard a gunshot, a woman's cry for help, then a second shot. Running to the sounds, one of them saw a black man standing over Meyer's body, his pants unzipped. Meyer had been killed instantly by a gunshot to the head.

Moments later police arrested a black man named Ray Crump near the scene. He was sopping wet and claimed he had gone in the river to retrieve a lost fishing pole (later found at his home). The eyewitness identified Crump as the man he'd seen with Meyer's body. The circumstantial case against Crump was strong, but the murder weapon was never found. Crump was eventually acquitted for lack of evidence.

Although Crump went on to a prodigious life of crime with twenty-two arrests in the Washington, DC, area, including assault with a deadly weapon, arson, and rape, the conspiracy theories sprouted like weeds. When news of her affair with JFK became known, some believed Meyer was killed by the CIA to cover up anything she might have known about his assassination. Some have even surmised it was the KGB. Nonetheless, Meyer's murder remains officially unsolved.

Mary was buried in her Milford hometown. As the niece of Pennsylvania Governor Gifford Pinchot, she grew up in his family mansion, Grey Towers, at 151 Grey Towers Drive in Milford (GPS 41.32842, -74.81463). No doubt enjoying the inside joke, JFK declared it a historic landmark in 1963, and his dedication plaque is still there.

Mary's ex-husband, renowned CIA operative Cord Meyer (1920–2001) is buried in Section 60, Site 7942 (GPS 38.87571, -77.06393) at Arlington National Cemetery.

See also *The Crime Buff's Guide to Outlaw Washington, DC* (Globe Pequot Press, 2012).

THE BLOODIED LINCOLN FLAG
Milford

The Pike County Historical Society is at 608 Broad Street, or GPS 41.32603, -74.79873.

On the evening of April 14, 1865, stage manager Thomas Gourlay of Ford's Theater in Washington, DC, was enjoying the play, *Our American Cousin*, in which his daughter Jeannie had a small role. At a big laugh-line, a shot rang out, mortally wounding President Abraham Lincoln. His assassin, John Wilkes Booth, leaped dramatically to the stage and escaped.

Gourlay raced to the president's side, grabbed the American flag that hung on the balcony of the presidential box, and placed it under Lincoln's bleeding head. When Lincoln was moved across the street to the Peterson boarding house, Gourlay retrieved the flag and kept it as a memento of the night his beloved president was assassinated.

Decades later his family donated it to the historical society, and it occupies the building's first floor, along with other Lincoln assassination memorabilia.

The flag that cradled Lincoln's bloody head at Ford's Theater

In 1804, Vice President Aaron Burr killed Alexander Hamilton in America's most famous duel.

AARON BURR'S HIDEOUT
New Hope

The Aaron Burr House Inn is at 80 West Bridge Street, or GPS 40.364000, -74.95503.

You might think politics are rough today, but at least politicians aren't shooting each other . . . yet. But that wasn't the case on July 12, 1804, when Vice President Aaron Burr faced off with dueling pistols against former Secretary of the Treasury Alexander Hamilton. The two had been feuding for some time, and scathing remarks made by Hamilton while Burr was running for governor of New York may have caused Burr to lose.

The Burr House Inn

Burr demanded a duel, and the two met on a cliff in Weehawken, New Jersey. Hamilton's shot missed, but Burr's didn't, mortally wounding Hamilton. Burr avoided arrest by hiding in the foundations of a friend's unfinished home until the coast was clear, then fled south. When no charges were filed, he returned to Washington, DC, and nonchalantly finished out his term in office.

Today, the foundations are all that remain of the colonial house, but a Victorian bed-and-breakfast now rests on top of them.

THE KILLER MILLIONAIRE
Newtown Square

The former John E. duPont estate, Foxcatcher Farm, is at the intersection of Goshen Road and North Newtown Street Road, or GPS 39.99660, -75.40814. The compound is private property.

The duPont family traced its wealth back to the Revolutionary War, when they founded the first successful gunpowder manufacturing company in America—an ominous portent for a twentieth-century descendant.

John duPont (1938–2010) was always a little "off," doing bizarre things like intentionally driving two of his Lincoln Continentals into the pond on his estate and shooting a cannon at the geese who gathered there because he thought they were "hexing" him.

As the years rolled by, his behavior grew increasingly erratic: taking the timers off his treadmill because he thought they were transporting him into the past; cutting his legs to release the bugs from outer space that were living in them; declaring himself to be the Dalai Lama of America; and believing Nazis were hiding in his trees, and ghosts were moving objects around in his palatial mansion. Ordinary people might be declared insane and institutionalized, but fabulously rich people are merely considered "eccentric" and are left alone.

John loved the Olympic Games and tried out for the swimming team, but he wasn't fast enough. So he decided to open up his farm as a training facility for Olympic wrestlers, among them 1984 Gold Medal winner, David Schultz. Schultz lived in a large guesthouse on the estate and practiced for the next Olympiad at duPont's state-of-the-art facility.

Things went smoothly until duPont's paranoia eventually took a weird turn. He suspected the wrestlers were plotting against him, so he started carrying guns. Confronting one of the athletes at riflepoint, he ordered him off the property. Worried, most of the others also packed up and left, but Schultz laughed off duPont's stunt and refused to go. It was a fatal decision.

*The guesthouse on the duPont estate where David Schultz
was murdered*

On January 26, 1996, duPont drove up to the guesthouse (now a
derelict mess) at 3901 Goshen Road (GPS 39.99127, -75.41766) and
shot Schultz to death. He then returned to his mansion and waited for
the police.

For two days cops surrounded the house and pleaded with duPont
to surrender, but he refused. After they turned the heat off in the mansion, duPont was arrested when he came outside to switch it back on.

The millionaire was found guilty but mentally ill and was sentenced to thirteen years in prison, with periodic stays in various mental
hospitals. He died in prison on December 9, 2010, at age seventy-two.
His personal wealth at the time of the murder was $250,000,000.

Today, a tiny view of the duPont mansion, which is mostly hidden by foliage, can be seen through the wire fence at GPS 39.99044,
-75.42165.

THE AMISH SCHOOLGIRL MASSACRE
Nickel Mines

The former Amish schoolhouse (torn down right after the crime) was at 4876 White Oak Road, or GPS 39.95979, -76.08453, across the street from the community swimming pool. This is private property.

On October 2, 2006, Charles Roberts IV, for reasons known only to him, entered a one-room Amish schoolhouse with a gun. Ordering the boys and the teacher to leave, he tied up the remaining ten girls, telling them if they did what he wanted he would let them go. He then called his wife on his cell phone and told her that he was getting revenge for the crib-death of their infant daughter in 1997 and would kill himself to atone for his molestation of his nieces twenty years before, an event the nieces later claimed never happened. She tried to talk him out of his terrible plan, but he wouldn't listen.

By then, the freed students and teacher had summoned help, and police and paramedics gathered at the school. Roberts called 911 and told the police dispatcher to make the cops back off; but before the dispatcher could warn the officers Roberts aimed his gun at the helpless girls. The oldest, thirteen-year-old Marian Fisher, probably hoping the others might be saved, told Roberts to shoot her first. He readily obliged, then went down the row and shot each child, before turning the gun on himself as the cops charged inside. Five of the girls were killed and the others were severely wounded. Ironically, on the school wall was a sign proclaiming, VISITORS BRIGHTEN PEOPLE'S DAYS.

The dead girls are buried near each other at the back of the Amish Cemetery, Quarry Road between Furnace and Haiti Roads, Bart Township, at GPS 39.93156, -76.08613. Mary Liz Miller and her sister, Lena, are at GPS 39.93125, -76.08698. Naomi Ebersole is at GPS 39.93150, -76.08705. Anna Mae Stoltzfus is at GPS 39.93139, -76.08706. And the brave Marian Fisher rests at GPS 39.93136, -76.08705.

Grave of Marian Fisher, who told the gunman, "Shoot me first"

Gunman Roberts is buried in an unmarked grave to the left of his infant daughter, Elise, at Georgetown United Methodist Church Cemetery, behind the church at 1074 Georgetown Road in Georgetown, Pennsylvania. Her grave has a heart-shaped pink marker at GPS 39.94003, -76.08534.

THE HEX MURDER
North Hopewell Township

The murder house still stands at 1709 Rehmeyer's Hollow Road, at GPS 39.80432, -76.65022. It's now owned by the great-grandson of Nelson Rehmeyer, who plans to turn it into a museum.

In the 1800s, some German immigrants combined their ancient healing arts with Native American beliefs, creating a new religion called Hexari. The practitioners of this religion, or *hexenmeisters*, were thought to have the ability to cast spells and curses on people and improve or ruin their lives.

In the 1920s, when John Blymire, Wilbert Hess, and John Curry experienced a string of bad luck, they believed someone was "hexing" them. Blymire sought the advice of the local seers to discover who the culprit might be, but no one could help him until he met Nellie Noll, aka "The River Witch of Marietta."

She told him that the man who had cursed him was Nelson Rehmeyer, a local *hexenmeister*, and that he could break the spell two ways: get Rehmeyer's copy of the spell-book, *Long Lost Friend*, and burn it, or bury a lock of Rehmeyer's hair six feet underground.

So Curry and Blymire went to Rehmeyer's house for a talk. Blymire tried unsuccessfully to telepathically will Rehmeyer into surrendering the book.

The next day, November 28, 1928, the men returned to Rehmeyer's home with Hess and stomped the *hexenmeister* to death. Unable to find the spell-book, they robbed their victim of ninety-seven cents and tried to burn the house down before they fled. The fire petered out, and Rehmeyer's body was discovered.

The three men were soon arrested for the crime. At their sensational trials Blymire and Curry received life in prison, and Hess got ten to twenty years.

Rehmeyer is buried at St. John's Lutheran Church Cemetery, 2944 Sadler's Church Road in Stewartstown. The grave is at GPS 39.77314, -76.63683.

"Hexenmeister" Nelson Rehmeyer was murdered inside this house.

JOSEPH SMITH: SINNER OR SAINT?
Oakland

The Smith homestead stood on Route 171, just west of State Route T840, at GPS 41.95135, -75.63879.

Joseph Smith, founder of the Mormon religion, started out as a con-man. After watching a self-proclaimed "diviner" in his Vermont hometown defraud some farmers by charging them three dollars per person per day to search for mysterious (and non-existent) hidden treasure on their farms, Smith decided to try the same ruse on the locals in the Susquehanna Valley.

During the "hunt," Smith stayed at the home of farmer Isaac Hale and fell in love with his daughter, Emma. When Smith asked for Emma's hand in marriage, Hale refused, believing his would-be

LDS founder Joseph Smith LIBRARY OF CONGRESS

son-in-law to be a worthless charlatan. He and the other swindled men filed charges against Smith, who was convicted of "disorderly conduct and being an imposter." No jail time was imposed.

Defying her father, Emma eloped with Smith. After a brief stay in Palmyra, New York, the newlyweds returned to Hale's farm, where they were given a small log cabin in exchange for Joseph's renouncing his treasure-seeking to live a responsible life of working on the farm.

Very little farm work was ever done, but in that cabin over the next two years, Joseph dictated the first draft of the Book of Mormon.

A new religion was born, and the Smiths moved away from Pennsylvania. But Mormonism didn't sit well with many Americans. In Missouri, twenty-two people were killed in anti-Mormon conflicts, and Smith's followers were expelled. By then Smith was practicing polygamy, taking as many as twenty-seven wives, some young enough to be his daughters.

In Illinois, too, Smith's group also wore out its welcome. Rumor had it that Smith wanted to establish a global theocracy with himself as king. Some of his own followers turned against him and published a critical newspaper, describing his megalomania and plural marriages.

In 1844, Smith ordered the printing press destroyed, bringing local citizens to arms. Declaring martial law, Smith called out his Mormon militia. But before blood was shed, the governor promised Smith safe passage to Carthage, where he would be fairly tried for inciting a riot. Smith agreed and was thrown into the Carthage jail but charged with treason, not rioting. Within days an angry anti-Mormon mob stormed the jail and shot Smith to death.

There is a park on the site of the Smith homestead with a statue and interpretive plaques. Just east of the park is the McKune Cemetery, where Smith's in-laws, Isaac and Elizabeth Hale, are buried (along with Joseph and Emma's infant son, Alvin). The cemetery is at GPS 41.95093, -75.63687. The graves are near each other in the sixth row from the back and close to the highway at about GPS 41.95083, -75.63669.

Joseph Smith (1805–1844) and wife, Emma (1804–1879), are buried in the Smith Family Cemetery in Nauvoo, Illinois.

JIHAD JANE
Pennsburg

The second-floor apartment is at 427 Main Street, or GPS 40.39765, -75.49673. This is private property.

If you conjure up the image of a radical Islamic terrorist, it's highly doubtful that forty-eight-year-old, five-foot-tall, blue-eyed, blond Colleen LaRose would be it. Yet, strange as it seems, she's

"Jihad Jane" recruited Islamic terrorists while living in this apartment building.

now in federal prison, having confessed to conspiring with terrorists, lying to the FBI, and attempted identity theft.

Born in Michigan and raised in Texas, LaRose was a hard-drinking, two-time-divorcee when she met Kurt Gorman, a Pennsylvanian who was visiting Texas on business in 2004. The two hit it off, and she agreed to move into his Pennsburg apartment and care for his ailing father while he worked.

Gorman saw nothing amiss during their five years together, and LaRose certainly never discussed Islam or attended a mosque. But while he was at work, she trolled the Internet under the alias "Jihad Jane," recruiting fellow extremists to help her kill Swedish cartoonist Lars Vilks, who had aroused Islamic ire by drawing Prophet Mohammad's head on a dog's body. She even pledged her own martyrdom in the cause of an Islamic holy war.

Gorman's father finally died, and the day after his funeral, October 16, 2009, LaRose disappeared—along with Gorman's passport. She flew to Europe to train with her jihadist cohorts to kill Vilks. While it isn't known if she ever got close, the FBI arrested her at the Philadelphia International Airport when she returned to the US, mission-unaccomplished. In 2011, she pleaded guilty to all charges and was sentenced to thirty years.

THE JOHNSTON GANG
Pennsbury Township

The killing field is south of Chadds Ford, on the left side of Crossart Road (unmarked), a few miles west of its intersection with Route 100, or GPS 39.84636, -75.60431. A cattle gate blocks access to the spot.

Three brothers—Bruce Johnston Sr., David Johnston, and Norman Johnston—along with their motley crew of other criminals, terrorized Chester County and its environs for years. Two of Bruce's sons and three of their young friends often joined the mayhem and called themselves the "Kiddie Gang." Mainly, they stole farm equipment, but they weren't above the occasional armed robbery, drug deal, arson, witness intimidation, rape, or murder.

The gang's reign of terror resulted in at least three hundred thefts and ten murders.

On November 15, 1972, policemen Bill Davis and Dick Posey were gunned down as they exited their cruiser in front of the police station, East Maple and North Broad Streets, Kennett Square (GPS 39.84765, -75.71079).

Gang member Gary Crouch testified against the Johnstons at a preliminary hearing, then disappeared on July 16, 1977. Many years later, another gang member led cops to Crouch's bullet-riddled body in the woods behind the historic Stottsville Inn, Timacula Road and Valley Road in Sadsbury (GPS 39.95905, -75.88855).

The Crouch testimony made the brothers paranoid about future snitches. They determined their weakest link was the "Kiddie Gang" and decided to eliminate them.

On August 16, 1978, they dug a large pit at a farm on Crossart Road and, one by one, lured three of the youths—including Bruce Johnston's stepson, Jimmy—to the site, under the pretext of stealing a tractor. As each boy came to the edge of the hole, one of the gang members shot him in the head and threw him into the pit. The gang rounded up a fourth and killed him at a landfill. His body was never found.

Now the only "Kiddie Gang" survivor was Bruce Johnston's son, Bruce Jr. Authorities offered him protection if he'd testify against his dad, and he eventually agreed.

But before protection could be arranged, Bruce Jr. and his girlfriend, Robin Miller, were attacked by two gunmen—believed to be his uncles—at her house at 256 Union Square Road in East Nottingham Township (GPS 39.76464, -76.02110). Junior was shot eight times but survived. Robin was killed.

Now more determined than ever to bring his father and uncles to justice, young Bruce testified against the gang. Along with other gang turncoats, his testimony ended the Johnston Gang's evil run. The three brothers were sentenced to life terms.

But, even in prison, no one was safe from the Johnstons. While Bruce Sr. served his time in the old, fortress-like Western Penitentiary, 1922 Westhall Street in Pittsburgh (GPS 40.47194, -80.04327), fellow prisoner George Arms filched some items from Bruce's cell. Bad idea.

On January 28, 1985, on Bruce's orders, inmate Jose Lopez squirted lighter fluid on Arms and set him ablaze with a match. Badly burned, Arms died a few agonizing months later. Even though other inmates saw the crime and testified, both Johnston and Lopez were acquitted.

The 1986 film *At Close Range*, starring Sean Penn and Christopher Walken, was loosely based on the Johnston Gang.

SUNDANCE KID'S CHILDHOOD HOME
Phoenixville

The house is at 354 Church Street, or GPS 40.13234, -75.52027. This is private property.

Before he became an Old West legend, Harry Longabaugh was the youngest of five children in this modest home. The nearby house where Harry was born (122 Jacobs Street in Mont Clare, at GPS 40.13656, -75.50709) was torn down long ago, although the surrounding homes remain.

Harry worked as a hired servant to a local family before leaving at age fifteen to seek adventure in the West. At age twenty, he grew tired of the cowboy's life and stole a horse in Crook County, Wyoming. Caught and convicted, he drew eighteen months at the Sundance jail—and got a new nickname. After his release, he never worked another honest day in his life.

In 1896, he teamed up with Robert Parker (alias "Butch Cassidy") and his "Wild Bunch." They robbed trains and banks until the Pinkertons made it too hot for them in America.

Childhood home of notorious train-robber, Harry Longabaugh, aka The Sundance Kid

In 1901, Butch and Sundance (with Sundance's girlfriend, a beautiful ex-teacher and ex-hooker named Etta Place) sailed to Argentina, then ultimately Bolivia, where they sustained themselves with ranching, mining, and robbery until they were reportedly ambushed at the small village of San Vicente by Bolivian *federales* after a 1908 payroll heist. Surrounded in a desperate gunfight, the two *gringos* were trapped. According to the troops, a grievously wounded Sundance was shot in the head by Butch, who then killed himself rather than be captured (not exactly a Hollywood ending). The corpses were buried together in an unmarked hole in the village graveyard (GPS 21.2642, -66.3155). They've never been positively identified, giving rise to several stories about how they survived and returned to the US to live out their lives quietly.

Harry's parents, Josiah and Annie Longabaugh, and his sister Emma are buried at Morris Cemetery, 428 Nutt Road in Phoenixville. The graves are in Section E, Lot 277, or GPS 40.12650, -75.52318.

In 1969, Paul Newman and Robert Redford starred in *Butch Cassidy and the Sundance Kid*, a romantic revision that bore little resemblance to facts but elevated the outlaws to the mythic stature of Robin Hood.

For more about Butch Cassidy, the Sundance Kid and the Wild Bunch, see *The Crime Buff's Guide to the Outlaw Rockies* (Globe Pequot Press, 2011).

Harry Longabaugh, aka The Sundance Kid, with Etta Place

Graves of Josiah and Annie Longabaugh, parents of The Sundance Kid

TIGER LIL'S BIG SCORE
Pottsville

The former Rich home is at 1801 Mahantongo Street, or GPS 40.67662, -76.21407. This is private property.

Lillian "Tiger Lil" Reis was a sultry showgirl at the swinging 1950s nightclub, the Celebrity Room, in Philadelphia (now a parking garage), where she had no trouble attracting male attention. Among her admirers was millionaire businessman Clyde "Bing" Miller, who became her sugar daddy even though Lil already had a boyfriend—mobster-wannabe Ralph "Junior" Staino.

When Miller's fortunes went south, so did Lil's interest. In an effort to impress her, Bing told her about a friend—wealthy coal-baron John Rich—who kept thousands of dollars in a home safe. Lillian's interest perked up, and she quickly shared the news with Staino and some local burglars known as the K&A Gang.

The gang—allegedly John Berkery, Vince Blaney, Robert Poulson, and Staino—waited until Rich was vacationing in Europe, then went to the house on August 7, 1959. The crooks hoped they'd find around $100,000, but the vault held much more: $478,000.

Lillian used her share to buy The Celebrity Room and ran it herself. The robbers went on a drunken spending spree in Atlantic City, then bought houses and cars.

Richie Blaney, Vince's brother, jailed for another offense, saw a get-out-of-jail-free card with what he knew of the Pottsville heist. He ratted on the burglars in exchange for his freedom. Very quickly, Lil and the boys were busted.

Vince and Poulson confessed immediately, implicating the others. While the gang was free on bail awaiting trial, Vince's corpse, with a bullet in its head, was found floating off the coast of Margate, New Jersey. He's buried in Beverly National Cemetery in Beverly, New Jersey, in Section X, 0, 794.

Similarly, Poulson was beaten, stabbed, shot in the head, and dumped on hospital grounds in Camden, New Jersey. Miraculously, he was found by the hospital staff and nursed back to health. But his memory of the Rich heist suddenly grew very fuzzy, and he refused to cooperate further with the police.

Snitch Richie Blaney got his due in true gangland fashion. On July 27, 1961, he left his home at 6011 Alma Street in Philadelphia (GPS 40.03518, -75.08261) and got behind the wheel of his Oldsmobile. As he turned the key, a bomb blew him to bits. He is also buried in Beverly National Cemetery in Beverly, New Jersey, in Section W, 0, 1629.

Tiger Lil went to trial, but the jury couldn't reach a decision. Her second trial resulted in a guilty verdict, but it was overturned on appeal. Weary of the whole case, the prosecutor dropped the charges and she was freed. In 2009, she died at age seventy-nine and is buried at Edlington Cemetery in Clarksboro, New Jersey.

DUTCH MARY AND THE MOB
Reading

Charles Evans Cemetery is at 1119 Centre Avenue. The grave is in Section 50, Lot 75, or GPS 40.35753, -75.93142.

Young Mary L. Gruber came to Reading to work as a domestic, but five dollars a week didn't go far, even before World War I. So she drifted into prostitution and, with superior management skills, soon became a madam known as Dutch Mary. Her brothel at 608 Cherry Street (now a modern building at GPS 40.33442, -75.92567) quickly became popular in eastern Pennsylvania and thrived for more than forty years. She was arrested so many times for prostitution offenses that the authorities resorted to putting ditto marks in her police record.

For many of those years, racketeers ruled Reading, profiting from human vices such as gambling, numbers, illegal booze, and prostitution. One of them, mobster Tony Moran, wanted a cut of Dutch Mary's business, but she rebuffed him. So Moran ordered the cops under his control to raid her constantly. Determined to get

Grave of notorious madam, Dutch Mary

even, Dutch Mary became an FBI informant and helped send Moran to prison briefly. When he got out he was even more intent to put Dutch Mary out of business.

Fortunately for her, Moran was murdered by one of his own lieutenants in 1945, but a corrupt mayor (and his mobster hench-man) finally shut Mary down for good in 1957 after she refused to play ball with them, too.

When her brothel was torn down during urban renewal, Read-ing citizens flocked to the site and grabbed whatever souvenirs they could find, including bricks, fixtures, and fireplace accessories. They are now proudly displayed in many area homes.

Mary died on August 14, 1959, at the age of eighty-seven. A party girl to the end, it's said she died falling off a bar stool and into the arms of a policeman. She's buried as Mary L. Quinn, next to her husband, John D. Quinn, who committed suicide in 1915.

THE HANGING OF SUSANNA COX
Reading

The Schneider/Geehr farm is still at 5798 Oley Turnpike Road, or GPS 40.34456, -75.80655. This is private property.

Sent into indentured servitude at age thirteen by her impoverished parents, Susanna Cox worked as a domestic for Daniel Schneider. At his death, his daughter Esther and her husband, Jacob Geehr, inherited the farm—along with servant girl Susanna.

On February 17, 1809, Jacob found the frozen remains of a newborn infant in a hole inside the wash-house. He confronted Susanna, who tearfully admitted that she had given birth three days before, but that the child was stillborn. Frightened, she'd hid the little corpse.

A justice of the peace and a doctor examined the child and determined it had been murdered. Susanna was arrested. In a trial that lasted less than five hours, the illiterate servant girl was not allowed to testify, nor were the proceedings translated into the only language she knew—German. Worse, the law at the time required at

Susanna Cox murdered her newborn infant inside this farmhouse.

least one witness to a stillbirth. Without a witness, the hiding of a dead baby was considered a sign of murder.

Susanna was convicted and sentenced to hang. She was taken to the Reading jail, where she continued to maintain her innocence. When hope for a reprieve was lost, she confessed to a clergyman that she had killed the child and hidden it in fear that the scandalized family would turn her out into the winter cold. She refused to name the baby's father and took his identity with her to the grave.

On June, 10, 1809, Susanna, wearing the only new dress she ever owned in her life, walked to the gallows behind a squad of soldiers and the wagon containing her coffin. A fife and drum played a dirge as the procession slowly moved up Penn Street toward City Park. An estimated throng of twenty thousand people watched from both sides of the street. Along the way, men and boys hawked broadsides containing mournful ballads about Susanna, and sympathy for her eventually became so great that she was the last woman hanged in Berks County.

At Gallows Hill (now a raised parking lot at GPS 40.33514, -75.91492), Susanna stood on the wagon and a rope was looped around her neck. After a short prayer and a hymn, the wagon pulled away and Susanna was "launched into eternity." She was buried on her sister's property in an unmarked grave at the intersection of modern-day Hampden Boulevard and Marion Street (now Hampden Park) in Reading (GPS 40.35299, -75.91014). During roadwork in 1905, her remains were found there but disappeared; the authors of *The Hanging of Susanna Cox* (2010) believe they were likely buried in an unmarked pauper's grave.

No record was ever made of her dead baby's burial.

Today, the Schneider/Geehr farm looks much as it did in 1809. The wash-house is gone, but the foundation with the hole remains and can be seen from the road in front of the house.

Every year, Susanna's hanging is re-created at the Kutztown Folk Festival. One of the old ballads is read aloud before a life-sized dummy is dropped through a gallows trapdoor.

A CALIFORNIA SERIAL KILLER'S VICTIM
Reading

Forest Hills Memorial Park is at 390 West Neversink Road. Mark Dreibelbis (1957–1973) has a small, in-ground marker in Section III, at GPS 40.30941, -75.89233.

Herbert Mullin was a California serial killer in the Santa Cruz area in 1972–1973. He believed his victims were giving him telepathic permission to sacrifice their lives so he could prevent a catastrophic earthquake from destroying the state.

He already had eight victims under his belt when, on February 10, 1973, he happened upon four youths camping inside Henry Cowell Redwoods State Park. One of them was Mark Dreibelbis, fifteen, a Pennsylvania police chief's son who had jumped bail to California to escape a marijuana charge. Dreibelbis and three teenage buddies had gone to the woods to enjoy their weed away from prying eyes. Pretending to be a park ranger, Mullin ordered them to leave. When the boys refused, he walked away, but returned a short time later to shoot them all to death.

Mullin would get one more victim before he was captured and sentenced to life in prison. Voted "Most Likely to Succeed" by his high school class, Mullin is eligible for parole in 2025, when he will be seventy-eight.

A BOOTLEGGER'S GRAVE
Reading area

Kesher Zion Cemetery is at 1051 Philadelphia Avenue in Shillington. The grave is in the front at GPS 40.29659, -75.93169.

Max Hassel was a small-time Prohibition beer-baron who tried to go big-time and was rewarded with a bullet.

Hassel started his empire in Reading, buying his first brewery at 2200 North 11th Street at the age of twenty-one. (The building still survives at GPS 40.36750, -75.91546.) He soon added two others, and the money flowed in as the beer flowed out. By age twenty-four, Max was a millionaire, buying his properties under fake names to fool the feds.

Not trusting the corrupt local cops, the state police raided Hassel's brewery at Third and Walnut Streets (now gone). They opened the tank valves and smashed barrels and bottles, unleashing a beer tidal-wave that threatened to drown some of the troopers. Beer poured out of the building and gushed into the streets, where thirsty neighbors reportedly scooped it up in buckets.

The IRS got involved, claiming Hassel's reported 1924 income of $21,000 was slightly off . . . by about a million bucks. The agency eventually settled for $150,000 in back taxes.

Hassel lived large—buying the Berkshire Hotel at 501 Washington Street (GPS 40.33700, -75.92779), where he occupied the top-floor penthouse. He also bought acreage in the countryside, where he built a retreat, complete with a lake and swimming pool, at 466 Golf Course Road in Birdsboro (GPS 40.23883, -75.89240), and created the nearby Green Hills Golf Course at 634 Golf Course Road (GPS 40.24463, -75.88819).

That might be enough for most men, but Hassel itched to play with the big boys in New York and New Jersey. So he bought and lived in the Carteret Hotel in Elizabeth, New Jersey—encroaching on the territories of Dutch Schultz and Meyer Lansky, two mobsters who didn't subscribe to Hassel's non-violent business model. When Hassel declined to pay them a cut of his bootlegging operations, it turned out to be "an offer he couldn't refuse."

On April 12, 1933, Hassel and partner Joseph "Big Maxie" Greenberg were gunned down inside Max's Carteret suite. Thousands attended Hassel's funeral. His death is officially unsolved, but on his deathbed in 2001, Lansky goon Joe Stassi hinted he was the killer. However, nobody was ever charged in the gangland murder.

A COLD CASE SOLVED
Reading area

The former Rupp home is at 4414 5th Avenue in Temple, or GPS 40.40195, -75.92531. This is private property.

From 1977 to 1982, serial killer Timothy Krajcir murdered at least eight women in the Midwest, and raped several more. But the former Pennsylvanian also committed a murder in his home state, a crime it would take nearly twenty years to solve.

On April 9, 1979, Krajcir peered into fifty-one-year-old Myrtle Rupp's window and liked what he saw. The next night he broke into the house and waited. But, when she arrived, she had her mother with her. Even though he had killed a mother and daughter before, he didn't have the stomach for it that night and escaped before the women saw him.

A week later, on April 16, 1979, he returned to the house and knocked on the door. Flashing a fake badge, he said he was investigating the earlier break-in. When Myrtle let him in, he grabbed her and steered her to the bedroom, where he tied her up, raped her, and strangled her.

The crime went unsolved until 2007, when DNA from the case led to Krajcir. To avoid the death penalty, Krajcir confessed to Rupp's murder and several other slayings. He's now serving thirteen consecutive life sentences in Illinois.

Rupp is buried at the Church of God Cemetery, 898 Suedberg Road in Suedberg. Her grave is at GPS 40.52761, -76.47110.

DEAD WIFE IN THE POOL
Reinholds

The former Roseboro home is at 107 West Main Street, or GPS 40.26575, -76.12024. This is private property.

In 2008, Michael Roseboro was a successful mortuary owner with a $500,000 annual income, a pretty, blonde wife, and four children. Their large custom-made corner home had an in-ground swimming pool with a cement patio and gas-powered tiki torches surrounding it. Life was good.

Well, maybe not really good. Michael was utterly besotted with Angela Funk, a married mother of two, whose house at 436 Walnut Street, Denver (GPS 40.23437, -76.13730) was just down the street from the Roseboro Funeral Home at 533 Walnut Street (GPS 40.23510, -76.13837).

Two months after their torrid affair began, Roseboro's wife, Jan, was dead. On July 22, 2008, she was found beaten, strangled, and drowned in the family pool.

Suspicion quickly fell on Michael when cops discovered 1,400 phone calls and 1,000 e-mails he'd exchanged with his lover. In the e-mails, Michael swore his undying love and proclaimed that the two of them would soon be together forever. And among their trysting spots was the funeral home.

Michael was convicted of Jan's murder and sentenced to life. Angela gave birth to Michael's son in March 2009, and is still living with her husband, the love-child, and her other children.

THE SKINHEAD MURDERS
Salisbury Township
The former Freeman home is at 1635 Ehrets Lane, or GPS 40.58761,-75.42049. This is private property.

Devout Jehovah's Witnesses, Dennis Freeman and his wife, Brenda, had tried to instill good values into their three sons, Bryan, David, and Erik. But as they grew older, Bryan and David chafed under the strict rules of their religion—no smoking, no drinking, and no celebrations or presents for Christmas or birthdays.

By their teens they had grown into sullen, rebellious hulks. They drank booze, took drugs, and got tattoos. With their cousin,

Benny Birdwell, they shaved off their hair and joined the neo-Nazi "skinhead" movement.

Their parents were at wit's end trying to bring their older sons back into the fold. Social-service agencies, church elders, and rehab did no good. Younger brother Erik lived in abject fear of his siblings, telling his aunt ominously, "You never know when you're going to die."

On February 26, 1995, Brenda Freeman was waiting when her two older sons and Birdwell sneaked in late after a wild night out. During a heated argument, Bryan stabbed his mother to death while his cousin allegedly bashed her with a metal pipe.

Past the point of no return, Bryan ordered Benny and David to arm themselves with an axe handle and baseball bat and to kill Dennis and Erik, who were sleeping peacefully upstairs. Dennis's head was crushed and his throat was cut, while Erik was beaten to death.

The three teens fled in the family car, getting as far as Michigan, where they took refuge with a white supremacist they'd met at a racist rally months earlier. They were arrested there.

By then the story of the murderous teenage skinheads had gone national, and reporters clamored to get their first look at the accused killers. They wouldn't be disappointed. At their arraignment, tall, stocky Bryan had a swastika tattooed on his neck and sported the word "Berserker" on his hairless forehead. David, even bigger, had a full red beard and a bald head with "Sieg Heil" inked on it. Benny, his chubby baby-face belying the darkness within, also had "Berserker" on his forehead.

Back in Pennsylvania, each blamed the others for the murders. But when the death penalty was taken off the table, Bryan and David confessed to the carnage and accepted life sentences without trial. Benny fought the charges but was convicted at trial and also sentenced to life.

See also "Another Teenager Runs Amok" (Lower Macungie Township).

A BELTWAY SNIPER VICTIM
Schwenksville

Christ Evangelical Congregational Church Cemetery is behind the church at 1132 Gravel Pike. The grave is at GPS 40.27487, -75.47828.

On October 9, 2002, Dean Meyers (1949–2002) was gassing up at a Sunoco station near Manassas, Virginia, when he was shot and killed—the seventh victim of the so-called Beltway Snipers, later identified as John Muhammad and Lee Malvo. Their shooting spree in Washington, DC, Virginia, and Maryland terrified the nation. Before the gunmen were captured, ten people would be dead and three others wounded. Ironically, Meyers had survived active-duty in Vietnam, only to be slain while pumping gas.

Meyers's murder was the case on which Muhammad was tried. Found guilty, he received the death penalty and was executed on November 10, 2009. Malvo, a minor, was given life in prison.

For more details, see *The Crime Buff's Guide to Outlaw Washington, DC* (Globe Pequot Press, 2012).

PATTY HEARST'S HIDEOUT
South Canaan

The farmhouse that became an SLA hiding place is at 54 Schott Road, or GPS 41.49775, -75.43392. This is private property.

In 1974, newspaper heiress Patricia Hearst became a kidnap victim, but she soon joined the radical group that had abducted her—the Symbionese Liberation Army. Calling herself "Tania" and toting a machine gun, she helped them rob banks and stores along the West Coast.

When the other radicals died in a burning house in Los Angeles after a shoot-out with police, Hearst and her keepers, Bill and Emily Harris, high-tailed it across the country and laid low in this rented farmhouse in rural Pennsylvania. They stayed a few

One of America's most famous fugitives, Patty Hearst, avoided capture by hiding in this unassuming farmhouse.

months before returning to California, where they were captured in San Francisco on September 18, 1975. Now living quietly as a mother and wife, Hearst received a seven-year sentence that was reduced to twenty-two months; the Harrises served eight years for the kidnapping.

THE PALMER RAIDS
Stroudsburg

Laurelwood Cemetery is at 904 West Bryant Street. Palmer's grave is in the Ridge Section, Room 3, or GPS 40.974807, -75.198574.

On June 2, 1919, a violent anarchist accidentally killed himself when he bombed the home of former Pennsylvania congressman and new US Attorney General A. Mitchell Palmer—part of a series of related attacks on government officials across the nation. The bomb exploded on Palmer's front porch, shattering windows but hurting nobody except the bomber himself.

The bombed house still exists at 2132 R Street NW, or GPS 38.912492, -77.048227. The blast rattled Palmer's neighbors, including the young Assistant Secretary of the Navy Franklin Delano Roosevelt and his wife, Eleanor, who lived across the street at 2131 R Street NW (GPS 38.912719, -77.048148).

The attacks sent a fearsome shudder through America, still edgy about the Bolshevik revolution in Russia, violent labor strikes, and a deadly flu pandemic that killed nearly a million Americans. Palmer, a possible presidential candidate in 1920, created a secretive intelligence bureau in the Justice Department and placed a young lawyer named J. Edgar Hoover in charge.

Within months, the new Bureau of Investigation was raiding lairs of suspected radicals and deporting "undesirables." Emboldened by his success and the recent Sedition Act, Hoover mounted a massive simultaneous raid on radicals in eight American cities in 1920 and arrested more than 6,000 suspected anarchists in one fell swoop. Although today's FBI credits the so-called Palmer Raids with providing valuable experience in intelligence-gathering and terrorism investigation, it also acknowledges the raids were fraught with obvious constitutional and civil-liberty missteps.

The ambitious Palmer (1872–1936) forged ahead, predicting that a communist revolution would erupt in the USA on May 1, 1920. The

American public panicked . . . but the revolution never materialized. Not surprisingly, Palmer failed to win the Democratic presidential nomination that year and largely became a footnote in history.

For more details, see *The Crime Buff's Guide to Outlaw Washington, DC* (Globe Pequot Press, 2012).

THE DEADLY DENTIST
Wilkes-Barre

The former Wolsieffer home is at 75 Birch Street, or GPS 41.24633, -75.90542. This is private property.

When Dr. E. Glen Wolsieffer told his wife Betty that he was going out with the boys, he didn't tell her that "the boys" were named Carol and Debbie. Enraged, Betty confided to a friend that she planned to confront him when he came home that night.

Early on the morning of August 30, 1986, Glen's brother Neil, who lived across the street at 84 Birch Street (GPS 41.24639, -75.90575), got an urgent phone call from Glen, telling him to come to the house. When Neil arrived, he found his brother on the kitchen floor, seemingly drifting in and out of consciousness. In his lucid moments, Glen claimed he'd been attacked by an intruder, who had choked him and knocked him out.

When cops and paramedics arrived, they found Betty's lifeless body on the floor of the upstairs master bedroom, savagely beaten and strangled. Glen was taken to the hospital while investigators searched the house. Right away, they noticed some strange inconsistencies: The ladder propped against the garage was turned backwards, making it difficult to climb, and the moss on the rungs was undisturbed. There were no footprints or dirt marks in the dew that covered the garage roof leading to the entry window and no indentations in the ground under the ladder's feet, indicating no weight had been put on it. They also saw that blood had been wiped off Betty's face, and her nightgown had been changed. Her expensive rings were still on her fingers, and nothing else was taken.

When they questioned the dentist in the hospital, he told them he had returned home from his night out, had a pleasant conversation with Betty, and then went to bed. Around dawn, he awoke to see a shadowy figure in the house. Grabbing his gun, he went downstairs, where he was jumped from behind.

Glen claimed he had struggled with his assailant, who had tried to strangle him from behind with a rope or chain. But the cops noticed that the ligature marks were on the back of his neck, not the front. Most suspicious of all, Glen's gun was still lying on the floor. Why would the robber not take it or use it on him? Then there was the overkill on Betty and only superficial wounds on Glen. And why did he call his brother instead of 911? Logic pointed at Glen, but hard evidence was scant.

Cops believed brother Neil knew more than he was telling, a charge Neil vigorously denied. On the day Neil agreed to undergo a polygraph exam at the county courthouse, Glen intercepted him at his house. What his brother told him will never be known, but at the appointed time for the polygraph, Neil drove past the courthouse and crossed into the opposite lane, driving head-on into an approaching eighteen-wheeler. He and his car were demolished. Neil is buried at St. Mary's Cemetery, 1594 South Main Street. The grave is at GPS 41.22129, -75.92004.

Three years later, Glen was tried and convicted of third-degree murder. He served thirteen years in prison and was paroled after he finally confessed to the killing.

Betty is buried at Mount Greenwood Cemetery, 40 South Pioneer Avenue in Shavertown. The grave is toward the bottom of the hill at the back of the cemetery, near the maintenance shed, or GPS 41.31131, -75.93636.

The book and made-for-TV movie, *Murder at 75 Birch*, was based on the case.

GEORGE BANKS'S MURDER SPREE
Wilkes-Barre

The Banks home was at 28 Schoolhouse Lane, or GPS 41.24772, -75.85831. It's now an empty lot surrounded by a wire fence. This is private property.

To say that George Banks's home-life was unusual would be an understatement. He was a black man living with three white girlfriends in the same house at the same time. His four young children—fathered with the three women—lived there, too, along with one woman's eleven-year-old daughter. Incredibly, a fourth white girlfriend and her son with Banks had also been part of this harem but had recently moved out to live with her mother, an act that might have triggered a deadly eruption.

On September 25, 1982, Banks woke up with a hangover. One child was in bed beside him, and his three girlfriends were dozing in chairs nearby, one with a child in her lap.

Banks grabbed his automatic rifle and started firing, killing all the women and children in the room. He then walked down the hall and shot the three remaining children to death.

Dressed in a Union Civil War cap, fatigues, and a T-shirt reading, "Kill 'em all, let God sort 'em out," he barreled out his front door. Seeing two men across the street, he fired at them, killing one and wounding the other.

He then drove to his fourth girlfriend's house at Heather Highlands Mobile Home Park, 109 South Main Street in Jenkins Township. Pulling up to the trailer on Lot 188, at the corner of East End Drive and Easy Lane (GPS 41.30043, -75.81675) and bursting inside, he shot and killed the woman, their child, her mother, and her nephew. Banks's body count was now thirteen dead—seven of them children.

Going to his mother's house, he told her what he'd done and begged her to drive him to an abandoned home at 24 Monroe Street in Wilkes-Barre (GPS 41.24019, -75.90016). She did as he asked but quickly called police, who negotiated with Banks for five hours until he surrendered.

He was convicted and sentenced to death. But when Banks's execution date came around, he was considered too insane to proceed. Now reportedly dying of liver cancer, he remains on Pennsylvania's death row.

RAGE IN THE RANKS
Wilkes-Barre

St. Mary's Cemetery is at 1594 South Main Street. The grave is at Lot 1, Range 9, East Section, or GPS 41.220779, -75.917938.

Navy Lieutenant (JG) Alton Grizzard had been a star quarterback for the Naval Academy. After graduation in 1991, he was assigned to the naval base in Coronado, California, where he met fellow Navy grads Ensigns Kerryn O'Neill and George Smith. While not romantically involved, Grizzard offered to walk O'Neill back to her apartment because she feared reprisals from Smith, a boyfriend she'd recently dumped.

Her fears were tragically well-founded. On December 1, 1993, Smith showed up at the apartment and shot Grizzard four times, then shot his ex-girlfriend in the head while she cowered behind a chair. Smith then shot himself.

O'Neill was buried in her native Wilkes-Barre, and Smith in Huntington Beach, California. The officer and gentleman Grizzard was laid to rest in Arlington National Cemetery (Section 59, Site 1192, or GPS 38.87770, -77.06543). "I thought he was the kind of kid the whole country would read about one day, but not like this," his high school football coach said.

For more details, see *The Crime Buff's Guide to Outlaw Washington, DC* (Globe Pequot Press, 2012).

THE WALKING PURCHASE SWINDLE
Wrightstown

The starting point is on SR 413 (Durham Road), just east of Penns Park Road, on the grounds of the Friends Meeting House, or GPS 40.26642, -74.98263. There's a tall historical monument and a large dedication boulder on the site.

One of the biggest land swindles in American history was committed by the son of Pennsylvania's founding father. William Penn, the proprietor of Pennsylvania, had always been fair and forthright in his dealings with the Lenni Lenape Indians who populated his land. The natives called him "brother," and peace prevailed in the province while Penn was alive. But, after his death, William's unscrupulous son, Thomas, was determined to cash in on the territory his father left him. He knew many new immigrants would pay handsomely for a piece of Pennsylvania.

Thomas produced a forged "treaty" he claimed had been negotiated between his father and the previous Lenape chief fifty years earlier that deeded to the Penn family all the Lenape territory a man could walk in a day and a half. Although suspicious, Lenape chief Nutimus cautiously agreed to honor the deal, reckoning that a man could walk about twenty miles in the allotted time.

But Thomas was sly. He had already cleared most of the land's obstacles and had hired three of the fastest runners in the colony to do the "walk." The men were promised five pounds each if they arrived at a predetermined point near present-day Jim Thorpe— nearly seventy miles away.

On September 19, 1737, they stepped up to the starting line. At the signal, they took off at full speed. The Indians protested, saying they were running, not walking, but their complaints fell on deaf ears. Two men dropped out; but one, Edward Marshall, made it all the way, flopping down exhausted at what is now State Route 903, two miles north of Jim Thorpe, or GPS 40.89529, -75.69041. (The historical marker that marked the spot is missing, but the

Thomas Penn's infamous land-grab began on this site.

pole and frame remain.) The land acquired was about the size of Rhode Island.

Realizing they'd been cheated, the Lenape appealed in vain to the King of England. The peace and tranquility so carefully cultivated by William Penn had been destroyed, thanks to what the Indians called, "Ye Hurry Walk." Even Ben Franklin denounced Thomas Penn as "a miserable churl."

The unrest caused by the Walking Purchase soon led to open warfare. Edward Marshall's wife and child became victims of a deadly Indian raid, and a marker stands at the former site of his home at the corner of Hester Street and North Delaware Drive in Portland (GPS 40.92118,-75.09571).

2

PHILADELPHIA METRO AREA

NANCY SPUNGEN'S GRAVE
Bensalem

King David Memorial Park is at 3594 Bristol Road. Nancy's grave is in Section BB, or GPS 40.13619, -74.94832.

Pennsylvania native Nancy Spungen (1958–1978) was a disturbed child who became an even more disturbed adult. Leaving home at seventeen, she knocked around Times Square for a while, working as a stripper before moving to London. She was a "punk rock" groupie, who wanted to hang out with and bed members of her favorite bands.

When she met Sex Pistols bass-guitarist John Ritchie, aka "Sid Vicious," they immediately hit it off and began living together. They soon moved to New York and lived at the Chelsea Hotel, spending their days getting high and wasted. The relationship eventually turned volatile, with screaming fits, rampant domestic abuse, and heroin addiction.

On October 12, 1978, Spungen was found in their bathroom stabbed in the abdomen by Ritchie's knife. He claimed he was so high he couldn't remember what happened. He was arrested for second-degree murder but made bail. While awaiting trial, Sid Vicious died of a massive heroin overdose. He was cremated, and his ashes were reportedly spread on Spungen's grave.

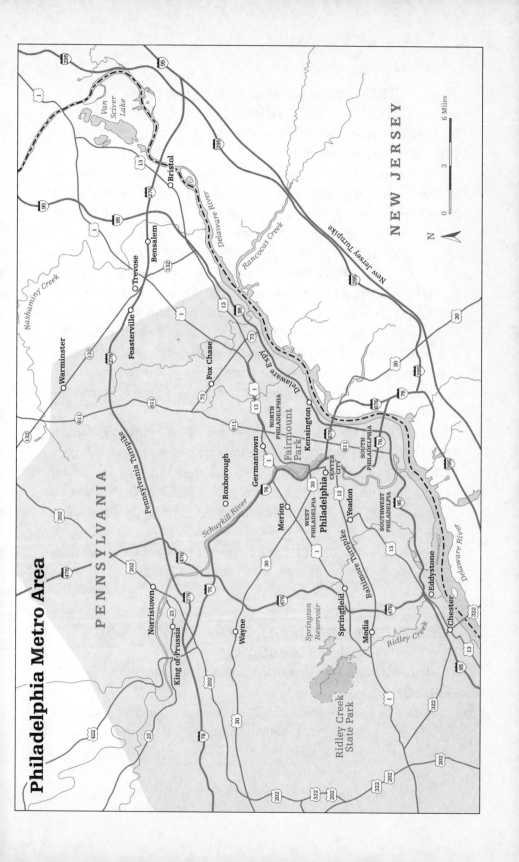

Philadelphia Metro Area

WHO KILLED CAROL ANN DOUGHERTY?
Bristol

St. Mark's Roman Catholic Church is at 1025 Radcliffe Street, or GPS 40.10014, -74.84586.

On October 22, 1962, nine-year-old Carol Ann Dougherty was riding her bike to the library, but she never made it. When she didn't come home by curfew, her parents went looking for her and found her bicycle on the front steps of St. Mark's Church. Rushing inside, her father discovered her raped and strangled body near the choir loft.

Investigators discovered that one of the parish priests, Father Joseph Sabadish, had been behaving rather bizarrely. He had gone to a neighborhood shoe store and asked if they sold underwear and had bought lingerie from another nearby store. He had also called a married woman and told her he wanted to rape her. After passing a polygraph test, he was quietly transferred to a different parish, and then transferred again and again to at least twelve more in the next eighteen years.

Decades later, when the uproar over pedophile priests erupted, it was revealed that Father Sabadish had been molesting children, both male and female, for years. By the time this was uncovered in 2004 he had already died. There was never enough evidence to charge him with Carol Ann's murder, and the crime remains unsolved to this day.

Father Sabadish (1918–1999) is buried in St. Mary Star of the Sea Cemetery (GPS 40.678174, -76.274190) in Llewellyn.

JOHN HENRY HOLLIDAY, DDS – "DOC" FOR SHORT
Center City

The Musical Fund Hall is at 808 Locust Street, or GPS 39.94698, -75.15507.

Before he became a legendary Old West gambler and gunfighter, John "Doc" Holliday (1851–1887) graduated with a dental degree

John Henry "Doc" Holliday

from the Pennsylvania College of Dental Surgery (now part of the University of Pennsylvania). At his commencement ceremony, he received his diploma inside this beautiful historic building, which also served as the site of the first Republican National Presidential Convention in 1856. He later opened a dental practice in Atlanta but was soon diagnosed with tuberculosis.

Believing the West's drier climate would be better for his health, he lit out for the territories. But the move proved not to be too healthy for the men who faced his gun. His reputation as a gunslinger was cemented forever after the gunfight at the O.K. Corral in Tombstone, Arizona, where he and the Earps made short work of the Clanton-McLaury gang.

As his health declined, Holliday moved to Colorado and died there at age thirty-six. His grave in Glenwood Springs's Linwood

Cemetery is lost, but a marker there (GPS 39.53962, -107.32057) reads, THIS MEMORIAL IS DEDICATED TO DOC HOLLIDAY WHO IS BURIED SOME PLACE IN THIS CEMETERY.

For more details, see *The Crime Buff's Guide to the Outlaw Rockies* (Globe Pequot Press, 2011).

THE DEVIL IN THE CITY OF BROTHERLY LOVE
Center City

The row-house where the murder happened stood at 1316 Callowhill Street, or GPS 39.95932, -75.16037. It's now a parking lot.

Herman Webster Mudgett (aka Dr. H. H. Holmes) wasn't America's first serial killer, but he was certainly the first to capture our nation's imagination through widespread media coverage. He admitted to twenty-seven slayings, but most crime-historians credit him with many more. His heinous acts began in Chicago, where he built a "Murder Castle" that served as a hotel during the World's Columbian Exposition of 1893. Many people checked in but never checked out—at least not in the way they had planned.

After authorities began to close in on Holmes in Chicago and Fort Worth, he morphed into a new incarnation in Pennsylvania. And he had a new plot.

Ben Pitezel was a handyman who'd helped Holmes in his criminal enterprises, which included bigamy, theft, fraud, and murder. Pitezel's large family and alcoholism required constant cash flow, so Holmes had little problem persuading him to be part of a scam in which they would insure Pitezel for $10,000, snatch a cadaver from a medical school, pass it off as Pitezel, and then split the insurance money. To set it up, Pitezel moved to Philadelphia to establish his identity there as B. F. Perry.

He found a room at a boarding house at 1002 Race Street (still standing but now an Asian market at GPS 39.95535, -75.15608), where he waited for Holmes to contact him. In August 1894, the two men

Ben Pitezel, H. H. Holmes's hapless handyman, first established himself in Philadelphia at this former boarding house.

met at a restaurant, where Pitezel confessed that he had forgotten to pay the insurance premium, and the grace period ended that day. An angry Holmes grabbed him and hurried to a telegraph office, where they wired the money just in time. If the unlucky Pitezel wasn't going to be a real cadaver before, he certainly was now.

They soon relocated Pitezel to the Callowhill Street building and opened it as a fake patent office. But less than a month later, on September 2, 1894, Holmes sneaked into Pitezel's room, where he was sleeping off a drunk, and forced chloroform down the helpless handyman's throat. He then drenched him in benzene and set him on fire, leaving broken glass behind to seem as if a patent experiment had gone awry and exploded in his face.

When news of Pitezel's strange death hit the papers, Holmes came forward to identify the body and collected his insurance money . . . but the narcissistic Holmes's web of lies quickly began to unravel.

A few months before, while Holmes was briefly held in the St. Louis Jail on fraud charges, he met Marion Hedgepeth, a notorious bank robber. Unable to resist confiding his insurance scheme to the robber, Holmes agreed to hire Hedgepeth's crooked lawyer, Jeptha Howe, to help him pull off the scam. In exchange for the "referral," Holmes promised Hedgepeth $500. When the pay-off never happened, the angry robber contacted the insurers and revealed the plot.

By then Holmes had absconded with the money and was leading his mistress and Pitezel's family on a merry chase around the country. As he went he coolly murdered three of Pitezel's children, telling their mother he had temporarily left them with a trusted friend. Pinkerton detectives finally ran Holmes to ground in Boston on the insurance-fraud case and returned him to Philly. But now the weird case was taking on a new life: Philadelphia Police Detective Frank Geyer wanted to know what had become of Pitezel's kids. After a tireless hunt he found the two girls' bodies in Canada and their brother's in Indiana. The news sent shockwaves across the country and led to a search of Holmes's Chicago "Murder Castle," where cops were horrified to find sealed rooms with gas-jets, a quick-lime pit, a dissecting table, acid vats, a large incinerator, trap-doors, and enough bones and clothing for two hundred people.

Holmes was tried for Pitezel's murder in Courtroom 676 of City Hall, Broad and Market Streets (GPS 39.95321, -75.16343). He was convicted and sent to Moyamensing Prison to await execution. The now-demolished prison once stood at the confluence of Reed Street, 11th Street, and Passyunk Avenue (GPS 39.93294, -75.16241), where a supermarket now stands. A low stone wall encircling the southern and rear sides of the market is all that remains of the old jail.

While waiting to be hanged, Holmes wrote his memoirs, a mixture of fact and fiction still in print today.

Holmes was hanged at the prison on May 7, 1896. To prevent grave-robbers and medical schools from snatching his body—a common practice in those days—he instructed his lawyer to encase his casket in concrete. But gravediggers poured the mortar into the coffin while it was on the burial wagon, before they got to the gravesite. When they arrived, they couldn't lift it out and, instead, pushed it off the cart, causing it to flip. As a result, the notorious monster likely lies face-down in his grave at GPS 39.92734, -75.25756 (although some of Holmes's descendants don't believe he's in that grave at all). See "Holy Cross Cemetery" (Yeadon).

After his death, some feared a "Holmes curse" when several key players suffered various mishaps:

- Linford Biles, the jury foreman at Holmes's trial, died in a freak accident on his roof in 1896 when tangled telegraph wires started a fire, and he was electrocuted while putting it out. His house still stands at 1031 Tasker Street (GPS 39.92980, -75.16261).

- Dr. William Mattern, the coroner who testified against Holmes, died suddenly of blood poisoning.

- Superintendent Perkins of Moyamensing Prison committed suicide.

- Father Henry McPake, who gave Holmes the last rites, accompanied him to the gallows, and officiated at his funeral, was found beaten to death in 1897 in the rear yard of St. Paul's Church, 10th and Christian Streets (GPS 39.93920, -75.15889).

- O. LaForrest Perry, the claims manager for the insurance company who set the Pinkertons on Holmes's trail, had his office gutted by fire. The only three things not burned were Holmes's arrest warrant and two photos of Holmes that the insurance man was keeping as souvenirs.

- Bank robber Marion Hedgepeth was pardoned by the governor of Missouri for his help in the Holmes case, but the robber soon returned to his old tricks. In 1910, he was shot to death by a cop as he held up a saloon in Chicago.

THE UNICORN KILLER
Center City

Ira Einhorn's former apartment is at 3411 Race Street, 2nd Floor, or GPS 39.95882, -75.19152. This is private property.

In the 1970s, smelly hippie guru Ira Einhorn called himself "The Unicorn" (because his German name translated to "one horn"). He had been a radical protester during the Vietnam War and became one of the founders of Earth Day. The burly, unkempt college professor hung out with counterculture figures like Allen Ginsberg and Abbie Hoffman, spewing New Age nonsense to lure naïve young girls to his bed.

One of them was Holly Maddux, a Texas girl who'd recently graduated from Bryn Mawr and moved into Einhorn's shabby Philadelphia apartment. They lived together for five years. But in 1977, Maddux had grown weary of her psychedelic lover's abuse and philandering and moved out. On September 19, 1977, Einhorn called her, threatening to throw out the possessions she'd left behind if she didn't return for them. She did . . . and disappeared.

The mummified remains of Holly Maddux were found inside Ira Einhorn's apartment.

On March 28, 1979, Holly's mummified remains were found stuffed in a trunk in a closet in Einhorn's apartment. Her skull had been viciously bashed, but she was sealed alive in the trunk. When detectives told Einhorn what they discovered, he said only, "You found what you found."

Out on bail while awaiting trial, Einhorn fled the United States in 1981; he was convicted in absentia in 1993 and sentenced to life in prison. Finally, in 2001, the fugitive Einhorn—free for almost twenty years—was extradited from France, reconvicted, and sentenced to life in a Pennsylvania prison. He's unlikely ever to be freed.

Holly Maddux is buried in her native Tyler, Texas, at Cathedral in the Pines Cemetery, 7825 South Broadway. The grave is in the Lake section, GPS 32.26369, -95.30858.

The story was retold in the 1998 made-for-TV movie *Peace, Love, Murder: The Ira Einhorn Story* and in Stephen Levy's 1988 book, *The Unicorn's Secret*.

AMERICA'S FIRST BANK ROBBERY
Center City

Carpenter's Hall is at 320 Chestnut Street, or GPS 39.94822, -75.14721.

In the late 1700s, the Bank of Pennsylvania was inside Carpenter's Hall, a trade-union building that's now a historical landmark. On August 31, 1798, Isaac Davis and Thomas Cunningham, two workers at the Hall, broke into the bank vault and stole $162,821.61

Historic Carpenter's Hall is the site of America's first bank robbery.

(more than two million in today's dollars). Police suspected it was an inside job and began questioning Hall employees.

A local blacksmith, Patrick Lyon, had been hired by the bank to work on the vault doors and to make a new key. He quickly finished the job and fled to the Delaware shore to avoid a deadly yellow fever outbreak. His access to the vault and his quick exit made authorities suspicious, and they declared him their chief suspect. Lyon indignantly returned to Philly to defend his good name and was immediately tossed into jail.

Meanwhile, one of the real robbers, Cunningham, had died of yellow fever, leaving cohort Davis to enjoy their ill-gotten gains alone.

None too smart, Davis began depositing big chunks of the stolen money into his bank account—at the Bank of Pennsylvania. His serial deposits aroused the bankers' curiosity, and when Davis was questioned, he promptly confessed, pledging to return all the money in exchange for no prison time. He gave back all but $2,000 of the cash, and America's first bank robber disappeared from history forever.

The falsely accused Lyon was released after spending three months in prison, and promptly sued the city (yes, even in 1798), settling out of court for $9,000. He then wrote a book with the unwieldy title, *Narrative of Patrick Lyon Who Suffered Three Months Severe Imprisonment in Philadelphia Gaol on Merely a Vague Suspicion of Being Concerned in a Robbery of the Bank of Pennsylvania with His Remarks Thereon* . . . a title that might be longer than his jail time.

AN HEIR'S DANGEROUS LIAISONS
Center City

The murder scene was inside Knight's apartment at The Dorchester, 226 West Rittenhouse Square, or GPS 39.94889, -75.17313. This is private property.

In 1975, young and charming John S. Knight III was the heir-apparent to his grandfather's vast Knight-Ridder newspaper empire.

But despite his trust-fund riches, the thirty-year-old Knight worked relatively low-paying jobs in the newsroom of Knight-Ridder's *Philadelphia Inquirer* just to get a feel for the journalism business.

Knight had a gift of gab, plenty of friends, and a $1,050-a-month apartment furnished with a $300,000 art collection. On December 7, 1975, he treated five buddies to a sumptuous dinner at a swanky Philly restaurant. After dinner three of the guests left for their homes, but Knight's old college roommate, Dr. John McKinnon, and McKinnon's wife, Rosemary, returned to their friend's luxurious apartment for a nightcap.

While Knight and the McKinnons chatted about old times, across town and a world away from the splendor of Rittenhouse Square, six drug addicts huddled in a squalid row house, getting high. Desperate for more drugs, they discussed how to score some quick and easy cash. One of the group, Isais "Felix" Melendez, suggested they roll the rich gay man he'd been seeing—John Knight.

Knight's friends had never suspected his hidden secret: He was a closet homosexual who, despite his wealth, roamed the seedy parts of town looking for male prostitutes. While walking on the wild side, he'd met Melendez, and the two "hooked up."

Around 1 a.m., McKinnon and his wife retired to a guest room for the night, while Knight went to his own bedroom.

A little later Melendez phoned Knight before he and two of his junkie buddies, Salvatore Soli and Steven Maleno, showed up at Knight's apartment with a gun. When Knight opened the door, the three overwhelmed him and tied him up, gagging him with his own expensive silk ties while they ransacked the apartment for money.

They found the McKinnons asleep. They took Rosemary out of the bedroom and tied her up while her husband slept. She watched Maleno and Soli leave with suitcases full of valuables. When Dr. McKinnon finally awoke, he overpowered the slight, wiry Melendez, who slithered free and ran from the apartment.

Meanwhile, Dr. McKinnon found Knight trussed up and unresponsive. The doctor untied his friend and tried to revive him, but Knight had been beaten severely and stabbed five times. He was dead.

Cops scoured the city for the killers. A few days later Melendez was found shot to death on a New Jersey golf course. Maleno voluntarily surrendered, and Soli was arrested soon after in Miami. Both blamed Melendez for Knight's murder, and Maleno admitted killing Melendez. At their trials they received life sentences.

Knight was buried near his childhood home in Columbus, Georgia.

ANNE MARIE FAHEY'S LAST MEAL
Center City

Ristorante Panorama is at 14 North Front Street, or GPS 39.95015, -75.14214.

Anne Marie Fahey, the twenty-eight-year-old scheduling secretary for the governor of Delaware, was tiring of her affair with prominent married lawyer, Thomas Capano, a former prosecutor and well-connected political figure. She decided to break off their relationship, but Capano didn't want to let her go. Even though he had several other mistresses, he couldn't tolerate losing control over Fahey.

On June 27, 1996, Capano convinced Fahey to have dinner with him so they could "talk." He took her to Ristorante Panorama, an exclusive Italian restaurant by the Delaware River. Their waitress noticed a coolness between the couple as she served their $154 meal. Fahey ate very little and spoke even less.

When they left the restaurant, Capano brought Fahey to his rented house in Wilmington, Delaware, and shot her in the head. He persuaded his brother, Gerry, to help him dump her body, stuffed in a cooler, in the Atlantic Ocean. They took Gerry's boat sixty-two miles from shore and pitched the cooler into the sea, but when it didn't sink, Capano shot holes in it. When it again failed to sink, Capano retrieved it and removed Fahey's body, then set the cooler adrift. Tying a chain around Fahey's body, he threw her overboard. The cooler, containing Fahey's DNA, was found by a fisherman and later used at Capano's trial.

Gerry broke under questioning by police, and Capano was arrested. During his murder trial another mistress, Debbie MacIntyre, told the court how Capano had persuaded her to buy a gun in her name and give it to him.

Even though Fahey's body was never found, Capano was convicted and sent to death row, but he died of heart disease in his cell on September 19, 2011, at age sixty-one.

Ann Rule's book and a TV movie titled *And Never Let Her Go* relate the Capano/Fahey story.

MURDER ON VIDEOTAPE
Center City

The post office is at 9th and Market Streets, or GPS 39.95064, -75.15534.

If you think somebody is always watching you, you're not paranoid; you might be right. Juan Covington found that out the hard way.

While working with pretty radiology technician Patricia McDermott at Pennsylvania Hospital, 800 Spruce Street (GPS 39.94579, -75.15591), Covington feared she was poisoning him with x-rays and decided to do something about it.

On May 17, 2005, as McDermott got off a city bus and strolled beside the post office, Covington approached her and shot her in the head, killing her instantly. He then calmly walked back to work.

When police scanned the security video at the post office, they saw the entire fatal encounter unfold before their eyes. Checking the *fifty* other cameras mounted on buildings along Covington's route, they found that they had followed the killer every step of the way on his trip to the hospital and inside the front door. He was identified by hospital personnel and arrested.

Under questioning, Covington confessed not only to McDermott's murder but to shooting four other people, two of whom died. He claimed to be ridding the world of "devils." Covington got three life terms in prison.

FATAL TRAFFIC VIOLATION
Center City

The murder scene is at the curb in front of 1234 Locust Street, or GPS 39.94784, -75.16207. This is private property.

As Patrolman Daniel Faulkner steered his police cruiser through downtown Philadelphia, he spotted a car driving the wrong way on a one-way street. After pulling over the driver, William Cook, Faulkner approached the vehicle to get his information. Cook jumped out of the car, and a fight ensued. Cook threw a punch at the policeman, who, in turn, struck him with his flashlight.

At that moment, William's brother, Wesley Cook (aka Mumia Abu-Jamal) happened to be walking on the opposite side of the street. Seeing the fight, the former Black Panther pulled his gun and charged at Faulkner, shooting him several times. As the officer crumpled to the ground, Jamal shot him four more times. Somehow retrieving his service revolver, the wounded Faulkner shot one round into Jamal's stomach before collapsing. More cops and ambulances sped to the scene, and the two wounded men were whisked off to the hospital.

Inside the emergency room, Jamal was overheard by several people screaming, "I shot the motherf---er, and I hope the mother-f---er dies!" Faulkner was pronounced dead soon after. He's buried at Glenwood Memorial Gardens, 2321 West Chester Pike, Broomall, in Section K, Lot 124, or GPS 39.98619, -75.35318.

Site of the fatal confrontation between Patrolman Daniel Faulkner and Mumia Abu-Jamal

Jamal got the death penalty, but he soon became a cause célèbre among college professors, liberal politicians, Hollywood notables, and even in France. His high-profile supporters believed he was an innocent political prisoner, persecuted by a racist society merely for his radical beliefs.

The facts in the case suggest otherwise. Bullets fired from his gun were found inside Faulkner, and the bullet extracted from Jamal's stomach was matched to Faulkner's gun. Several witnesses identified him as the shooter, and even his own brother wouldn't exonerate him. And he confessed.

Nevertheless, after a marathon of appeals lasting more than twenty years, his death sentence was commuted to life.

A plaque dedicated to Faulkner is set into the sidewalk at the scene of the crime, and several miles of Roosevelt Boulevard have been named in his honor.

THE VIDOCQ SOCIETY
Center City

Society headquarters is at 1704 Locust Street, or GPS 39.94877, -75.16962.

Named after French criminal-turned-detective, Eugene Francois Vidocq, who pioneered the use of forensics to solve crimes, these volunteers from the ranks of retired or active law enforcement meet once a month in Philadelphia to decipher cold cases. The society was founded by federal customs agent William Fleisher, forensic sculptor Frank Bender, and criminal profiler Richard Walter.

Their meetings convene in local historic taverns where, after a sumptuous meal, an unresolved case is presented to the assembled group, which then suggests new avenues for investigators to pursue. Their endeavors have closed many seemingly unsolvable crimes, such as the torture/murder of Scott Dunn by his girlfriend, Leisha Hamilton, in Lubbock, Texas, and the brutal murder of Terri Brooks by Scott Keefe in Bucks County, a case that had been cold for fourteen years.

No fee is ever charged for their services.

The book *The Murder Room* by Michael Capuzzo is about the Vidocq Society.

FRANK BENDER'S SCULPTING STUDIO
Center City

The former home and studio is at 2215 South Street, or GPS 39.94540, -75.17913. This is private property.

Westfield, New Jersey, detectives were down to their last hope of solving a crime that had stuck in their craw for eighteen years—John

List's slaughter of his entire family. The bodies of his wife, his mother, and his three children were found in the ballroom of their house in 1971. They had all been shot to death. Then List disappeared.

With only an old photograph of the fugitive, they sought sculptor Frank Bender's help to make a bust of what List might look like at the present time.

When finished, the sculpture was shown on TV's *America's Most Wanted*, where it was immediately recognized by a Colorado woman who knew the man, not as John List, but as "Bob Clarke." She called the show and gave authorities List's new address in Virginia, where he was captured without incident. When the real List was compared to the bust, the resemblance was uncanny.

Bender had found a calling as a forensic sculptor and began making casts of unidentified crime victims, working with just a skull to bring a face to life. Many formerly unclaimed skeletons were returned to their loved ones for proper burial, thanks to his efforts.

Even when diagnosed with fatal mesothelioma, Bender worked until he died on July 28, 2011. The Vietnam veteran is buried at Washington Crossing National Cemetery in Newtown. His grave is in Section 1, Site 753, at GPS 40.265470, -74.904484.

EASTERN STATE PENITENTIARY
Center City
The massive structure looms over 2124 Fairmont Avenue, or GPS 39.96737, -75.17274. It's open 10 a.m. to 5 p.m. every day (except major holidays), and tours are available. Admission is charged.

Built in 1829, this gothic edifice is considered to be the first modern prison in America. Its revolutionary wheel-spoke design was copied by more than three hundred prisons worldwide. Closed in 1971, it's been maintained as a "stabilized ruin" and is now a tourist attraction. With gargoyles guarding its gates, at Halloween it's transformed into a scary and popular "haunted house."

The fortress-like façade of Eastern State Penitentiary

Prisoner #1 was Charles Williams, who had stolen about twenty-five dollars worth of goods and was sentenced to two years' confinement. After him, many well-known criminals served time there, including murderer Bruce Johnston Sr., bank robber Willie Sutton, kidnapping conspirator William Westervelt, teenage psychopath Seymour Levin, and several of the so-called "Molly Maguires" who had managed to avoid the hangman.

But, undoubtedly, its most famous prisoner was Al Capone. On May 16, 1929, Capone and three of his henchmen were driving to New York, after meeting with other crime bosses in Atlantic City. When their car broke down in Camden, New Jersey, they took a train from there into Philadelphia and purchased tickets for another train to Chicago. That train wasn't leaving for several hours, so they decided to kill time by catching a movie.

As they walked into the theater, they were spotted by two Philly cops, who recognized the mobster and thought he might be up to no good. The policemen entered the lobby and waited for Capone and his party to come out. When the gangsters emerged, the cops flashed their badges, and Capone reached for a gun in his pocket.

Scarface was convicted of carrying a concealed weapon and sentenced to a year in the penitentiary. Compared to the Spartan cells of the other inmates, which consisted of a toilet, a hard bed, and a skylight in the roof affording the only light, Capone's was luxurious. It had lamps, a feather bed, a wooden desk, paintings, an oriental rug, an easy chair, and a cabinet radio. The warden also allowed Capone to use his telephone.

When he was released eight months later, Capone invited the prison guards to visit him in Chicago, where he promised to show them a good time (and some reportedly took him up on his offer). Capone's cell has been preserved exactly the way he left it and can be seen on the tour.

EDGAR ALLAN POE HOUSE
Center City

The house is at 532 North 7th Street, or GPS 39.96197, -75.14979. It's a National Historic Site, open 9 a.m. to 5 p.m. Wednesday through Sunday. Admission is free, and tours are available. Note the statue of a raven in the side yard.

If you love mystery books, you owe a debt of gratitude (or maybe a red rose and a bottle of cognac) to Edgar Allan Poe, recognized as the father of crime fiction. His 1841 story, "Murders in the Rue Morgue," introduced the literary world to the first fictional sleuth and many of the conventions still observed by today's modern mystery writers. Poe was a melancholy soul whose genius was not recognized until well after his death.

The world's first mystery author, Edgar Allan Poe, once lived in this house.

Always chasing the elusive fortune, he moved frequently. His time in Philadelphia was one of his most creative periods. Thirty-one stories and poems were published or written while Poe lived here, including some of his most famous, such as "The Black Cat," "The Pit and the Pendulum," "The Tell-Tale Heart," and "The Raven." Even his classic "Murders in the Rue Morgue" was written in Philadelphia.

The three-story brick house itself is tidy and unfurnished. In Poe's time it sat in a predominantly Quaker neighborhood. Poe lived there with his wife and mother-in-law for a year or less around 1843.

On October 3, 1849—Election Day—a friend found a delirious, incoherent Poe lying on the sidewalk outside a tavern at Gunner's Hall, 44 East Lombard Street in Baltimore (no longer existing at GPS 39.287833, -76.613901). Babbling and wearing someone else's clothes, Poe was taken inside the tavern briefly, then to Baltimore City and Marine Hospital (now Church Home Building) at 100 North Broadway, or GPS 39.293032, -76.594164.

Four days later, Poe died without ever regaining clarity. His death, which was subtly attributed to alcoholism, remains a mystery, but modern forensic investigators have surmised he might have been killed by epilepsy, heart disease, meningitis, syphilis, or even rabies. Others have speculated that he might have been the victim of "cooping," a form of election fraud in which reluctant dupes are forced to vote repeatedly—and to drink a lot of liquor.

Poe is buried in Baltimore's Westminster Burying Ground, 519 West Fayette Street. His current grave is at GPS 39.29018, -76.62358, although his original burial site was behind the church in the same cemetery at GPS 39.28981, -76.62313.

For more about Poe, see *The Crime Buff's Guide to Outlaw Washington, DC* (Globe Pequot Press, 2012).

PREGNANT AND MURDERED
Chester

The body was found in a small clump of trees and bushes in the parking lot of a large brown industrial building, just north of the intersection of West 4th and Palmer Streets, at GPS 39.83536, -75.38855.

She was a beautiful young woman with a radiant smile and was five months pregnant when she mysteriously vanished from her neighborhood. Sound familiar?

While reporters clamored to wring every last morsel out of the Laci Peterson case in California, the tale of twenty-four-year-old

Latoyia Figueroa, whose circumstances were similar, barely rated a back-page paragraph in one Philly newspaper. She became a victim of what some were calling "missing white woman syndrome," where only pretty Caucasian girls' cases were covered at the expense of minority victims. Local bloggers sought to remedy that situation by bombarding the networks with e-mails and shaming them into reporting the story. It worked.

Figueroa was last seen alive on July 18, 2005, with her boyfriend (also the father of her unborn child), Stephen Poaches, near South 59th Street and Walton Avenue in West Philadelphia (GPS 39.95122, -75.24090). Cops were called when she didn't show up for work and didn't answer her cell phone.

Investigators discovered that Poaches had a new girlfriend and was no longer interested in Latoyia. He'd begged her to get an abortion, but she'd refused.

Despite an intensive search, Figueroa stayed missing until August 20, 2005, when the new-found publicity made Poaches nervous. Thanks to a police tracking device, he was caught red-handed at the dump site as he attempted to move Figueroa's body. Poaches confessed he'd strangled her during an argument in his apartment. He was convicted and sentenced to life in prison.

Figueroa (1981–2005) is buried at West Laurel Hill Cemetery, 215 Belmont Avenue in Bala Cynwyd. Her grave is in the South Lawn Section, Grave 752, at GPS 40.01132, -75.22511.

It was unmarked for several years, but a headstone has reportedly been ordered.

Also at West Laurel Hill Cemetery:

- **Dr. David Hayes Agnew** (1818–1892), who operated on President James Garfield after he was shot by Charles Guiteau on July 2, 1881. He and the other doctors who attended Garfield stuck their germy fingers and instruments into the president's wound, inadvertently introducing a massive infection that finally killed him two months after the shooting. At his trial Guiteau actually blamed Garfield's doctors for his death, insisting that he only wounded him. The ploy didn't work, and Guiteau was hanged for the crime. Agnew is buried in a mausoleum in the Ashland Section, at GPS 40.01662, -75.22133.

THE WITCH OF RIDLEY CREEK
Eddystone
The Mattson farm once encompassed the entire area occupied by the present-day Peco Energy plant at 9th and Simpson Streets, or GPS 39.86049, -75.34048. This is private property.

Margaret Mattson was the principal figure of the one and only witch trial held in Pennsylvania. She was accused by her neighbors, and even her own daughter, of bewitching the cattle on the farms surrounding her property.

On December 21, 1683, nine years before the infamous witch trials in Salem, Massachusetts, Margaret stood before a judge's panel led by William Penn to defend herself against the witchcraft charges. As was the case in some of the Salem trials, accusations of this sort were usually an attempt by unscrupulous individuals to get their hands on valuable property, and the farm owned by Mattson and her husband, Nels, was one of the largest in the territory. Margaret, a Swedish immigrant who spoke and understood little English, wasn't much help in her defense and sometimes blurted out strange replies to the questions.

The jurors, suspecting the accusers' motives, reached a compromise verdict: "Guilty of having the common fame of a witch, but not guilty in manner and form as she stands indicted." Penn followed by asking Margaret if she rode a broomstick, to which she, misunderstanding, replied, "Yes." Penn declared that it wasn't against the law to ride a broomstick and fined her one hundred pounds to ensure her future good behavior.

BENEDICT ARNOLD'S PARTY HOUSE
Fairmont Park

The former Arnold home is at 3800 Mount Pleasant Drive, or GPS 39.98340, -75.19960. It's open for tours.

Before his name became synonymous with "traitor," Benedict Arnold was a hero. During the Revolutionary War, he showed immense courage and excellent strategic ability in capturing Fort Ticonderoga and winning the Battle of Saratoga, which forced the surrender of British General Burgoyne.

Arnold received two severe wounds in his leg in these battles. But, in spite of his derring-do, he was passed over for promotions, mainly due to his temper tantrums with his superior officers. His one great champion was George Washington, who appointed Arnold as commander of the city of Philadelphia after the British withdrawal.

Soon after his appointment, Arnold's political enemies accused him of war-profiteering and brought him up on charges before a court-martial, but he was acquitted. By then, he was married to beautiful socialite Peggy Shippen, for whom he bought the substantial estate in Fairmont Park, where they held lavish parties for their friends. Peggy was a British sympathizer, previously linked romantically to English spy Major John Andre.

Peggy had kept up a correspondence with Andre and encouraged Arnold to meet with him. But Arnold maintained his loyalty to his country until the Continental Congress claimed Arnold owed the government one thousand pounds for failing to account for his expenses while fighting in Canada. It was the last straw.

In his new position as commander of West Point, Arnold plotted with Andre to turn it over to the British in exchange for twenty thousand pounds and the rank of brigadier general in the English army. But, before the plan could be carried out, Andre was captured and hanged in Tarrytown, New York, and the scheme was exposed. Knowing the jig was up, Arnold joined the British army and won some victories for them in Virginia before moving to England. He died there on June 14, 1801, and was buried with full honors in St. Mary Churchyard in London.

THE KIDNAPPING HOAX
Feasterville-Trevose

The former Sweeten home is at 1941 Saxon Drive, or GPS 40.15839, -74.97768. This is private property.

The nation was gripped with fear as the story broke on May 26, 2009. Suburban mom Bonnie Sweeten was calling on her cell phone from the trunk of her car, telling operators that she and her nine-year-old daughter had been kidnapped by two black men. She claimed they had rammed her car, thrown them in the trunk, and sped off. The phone kept disconnecting, but she called back, more hysterical each time, until the line finally went dead.

A fleet of police cars tore through the streets of Philadelphia, pulling over every black Cadillac they saw. Amber alerts were issued, the FBI was called, and bulletins were sent all around the area. But the next day, mother and daughter were found alive and well at Disney World.

No kidnapping had occurred. Sweeten had been on the way to the Philadelphia airport when she called 911.

Worse, further digging revealed she'd stolen $280,000 from an elderly relative with dementia and embezzled $640,000 from a law firm where she'd worked. The money paid for the lifestyle Sweeten craved—a large home, expensive trips, and in-vitro fertilization treatments. When it seemed she might be prosecuted for the thefts, she tried to disappear in a kidnapping hoax.

Besides a year in jail for her false 911 call, Sweeten was sentenced to 100 months in federal prison for the thefts.

THE BOY IN THE BOX
Fox Chase

The discovery site is now the middle of the street across from 716 Susquehanna Road and in line with the telephone pole, or GPS 40.08255, -75.07236. In 1957 this was an isolated area, and the road was unpaved and half of today's width.

Grave of the unidentified child known only as "The Boy in the Box"

On February 25, 1957, a college student parked his car on secluded Susquehanna Road. He had previously been caught spying on the "wayward girls" at a nearby group home. So today (he'd tell police later) he was merely chasing a rabbit into the woods when he stumbled upon a large cardboard box containing the body of a young boy.

The child was around five years old, naked, and covered with a blanket. He had suffered from malnutrition, and his head showed signs of recent trauma. The skin on one hand and one leg had shriveled from immersion in water while alive. At least three scars suggested he'd had surgeries. His fingernails and toenails were neatly trimmed. But he had no identification.

Cops circulated posters seeking the boy's name and anything else they might learn about him. A long parade of people came to see the child, but no one knew him. Despite a heroic effort the boy remained unrecognized and unclaimed. Before long he was buried in a pauper's grave.

Over the years the case tugged the heartstrings of the detectives assigned to it. As each retired, he handed it off to the next, who tried just as diligently (and unsuccessfully) to give the child a name and justice. The mystery has never been solved.

In 1998, police and the Vidocq Society raised money to re-bury the child in a proper grave at Ivy Hill Cemetery, 1201 Easton Road, Philadelphia, beneath a traffic island near the front entrance at GPS 40.07430, -75.17841. His large tombstone reads, "America's Unknown Child." A smaller stone in front that had once marked his original pauper's grave states, "Heavenly Father, Bless This Unknown Boy."

Also at Ivy Hill:

- **Franklin B. Gowen,** the man who destroyed the "Molly Maguires." He's at GPS 40.07407, -75.18168. See also the "Molly Maguires" chapter.

THE BEATING OF EDDIE POLEC
Fox Chase

The crime scene is on the steps of St. Cecelia's Church, 525 Rhawn Street, or GPS 40.07598, -75.08072.

On November 11, 1994, sixteen-year-old Eddie Polec had no idea a rumble was brewing as he waited for his brother near the local McDonald's at the corner of Hasbrook and Oxford Avenues (GPS 40.07404, -75.08469). Rival gangs from Abington and Fox Chase planned to fight.

When the Abington kids arrived wielding baseball bats, the Fox Chase group scattered, running right past Polec, who ran too when he spotted the angry teenagers heading his way. The Abington mob caught up with him when he tripped on the church steps. They beat him ferociously, ignoring his pleas that he was merely an innocent bystander.

At least eighteen neighbors called 911 to report the melee, but it took police forty minutes to respond. By then, it was too late for Polec. His skull fractured in seven places, the teenager died where he fell.

When the 911 calls were reviewed, they revealed quarrelsome dispatchers had been more interested in doling out attitude than sending help. They yelled at and rebuked the callers, and some dispatchers had even hung up on them. The dispatchers were fired but sued to get their jobs back. Embarrassed by the debacle, the mayor of Philadelphia vowed a complete overhaul of the 911 system, including better training for the emergency workers.

All seven of Polec's killers were caught. Although convicted, each was paroled by 2011.

Polec is buried in Our Lady of Grace Cemetery, on an access road off Route 1 in Penndel. The grave is in Section 16, Range 6, Plot 22, Grave 2, at GPS 40.16544, -74.93470.

LITTLE CHARLEY ROSS
AMERICA'S FIRST CHILD ABDUCTION FOR RANSOM
Germantown

The Ross home has been torn down, and the Zion Hill Church of God now occupies its lot at 529 Washington Lane, or GPS 40.04994, -75.17413. All that remains from the time the Rosses lived there is the stone wall in front of the church.

Long before the Lindbergh baby, Adam Walsh, and Etan Patz, there was little Charley Ross.

On July 1, 1874, Charley, age four, was playing with his six-year-old brother Walter on the sidewalk near the wall in front of his house. Two men in a wagon rolled up and asked if they'd like to get some fireworks for the upcoming Fourth of July celebration. Since the men had stopped by earlier that week and given the boys candy, the brothers trusted them and climbed into the wagon.

The men took them to Kensington and stopped at a store. Giving Walter a quarter to get the fireworks, they said they would wait for him outside. But when Walter emerged with his goodies, the wagon, the men, and his brother were gone. A passerby took the weeping child home, where his frantic father, Christian Ross, had been combing the neighborhood looking for his sons. When Christian asked Walter where Charley was, he was told, "in the wagon."

A massive search was launched, but the boy was gone.

On July 4, 1874, a poorly written ransom letter arrived at Ross's dry-goods store at 304 Market Street (GPS 39.95008, -75.14601). Charley's kidnappers demanded $20,000 and warned that the boy would be killed if Christian refused to pay or called the police. But the police were already involved and advised Ross not to pay anything, fearing it would spark other kidnappings. Until then America had never had a child abducted for ransom, a malady that had plagued Europe for years.

Instead cops told the distraught father to play along until they could find Charley on their own. Giving him scripts of what to

Charley Ross was last seen by neighbors in front of this wall.

say, the police helped Christian communicate with the kidnappers through ads in newspapers addressed to "John," as the letter had instructed. He stalled for time, but with each delay, the kidnappers became increasingly hostile.

While searchers scoured the city for clues, reporters were having a field day. The kidnapping became a media sensation. Charley sightings were reported everywhere, and each one was baseless.

After twenty-three letters and ads in reply, Ross couldn't take it anymore. Ignoring the police, he sent representatives with the money to meet the kidnappers at a hotel in New York. The kidnappers never showed, the letters stopped coming, and all communication ceased. Charley was irretrievably gone.

But the fascination with the missing child continued. Newspapers followed the story daily. Con artists came out of the woodwork, promising they could return Charley for the right price. Foundling homes and orphanages offered various kids as the lost boy, but none of these "Charleys" could answer the personal questions the Rosses had supplied.

Meanwhile, tipster Gil Mosher told New York police that his brother William and a friend, Joseph Douglas, might be the kidnappers. Months before, they had tried to rope him into a scheme to nab a grandchild of shipping magnate Cornelius Vanderbilt and ransom the child for $50,000. When Gil turned them down, they disappeared, possibly to Philadelphia.

When experts compared William's known handwriting to the kidnap notes, they were declared a match. A massive dragnet was launched to find the elusive pair.

Philadelphia investigators tracked the two ex-cons to a rented house at 235 Monroe Street (GPS 39.93961, -75.14736), where they had lived until recently with a disgraced former cop named William Westervelt. After the Philly police chief declared he was ordering a search of every house in the city, all three fled back to their native New York City.

Westervelt later denied being involved in Charley Ross's kidnapping but fingered Mosher and Douglas.

On December 13, 1874, two burglars were shot by neighbors as they left an empty Long Island house they'd robbed. It was Mosher and Douglas. One was killed and the other mortally wounded. With his dying breaths, Douglas confessed to kidnapping Charley Ross but declared he didn't know where Charley was being held, that only the dead Mosher knew. The seemingly repentant Douglas said he was certain Charley would be released soon, and then died.

Through the years, more than 570 boys and young men came forward claiming to be Charley, but all were imposters. Charley was never found, dead or alive.

Westervelt was tried for kidnapping, extortion, and conspiracy, but convicted only on the last two counts. He served six years in Eastern State Penitentiary.

Christian and Sarah Ross never stopped searching for their son until their deaths. They spent an estimated $60,000 (over $1.5 million today) hunting for Charley. Christian regretted to his dying day that he hadn't paid the ransom right away.

It's believed the Ross case gave rise to the old familiar parental warning, "Don't take candy from strangers." And a major missing-persons database is named for Charley (www.charleyproject.org).

Brother Walter Ross grew up to become a successful business-man and lived in a huge mansion at 7924 Lincoln Drive (GPS 40.06707, -75.20308), in the exclusive Chestnut Hill section of Philadelphia, until his death in 1943. He's buried with his wife and children at St. Thomas Episcopal Church Cemetery, 600 Bethlehem Pike in Flour-town. His grave is in Section I, Lot 402, at GPS 40.12035, 75.21553.

The elder Rosses and their other children are buried at North-wood Cemetery, North 15th Street and 71st Avenue in Philadelphia. The family plot is at GPS 40.05996, -75.14374.

Also buried at Northwood:

- **William "Kid" Gleason** (1866–1933), manager of the 1919 Chicago White Sox, who famously "threw" the World Series, earning the nickname "The Black Sox." Despite claims otherwise, it is generally accepted that Gleason knew nothing of the scheme. His grave is about 100 feet behind and to the left of the cemetery office at GPS 40.06204, -75.14336. (Another Black Sox connection to Pennsylvania: George "Buck" Weaver, one of the eight banned players, was born in Pottstown in 1890.)

ATOMIC SPY HARRY GOLD'S GRAVE
The Great Northeast

Har Nebo Cemetery is at 6001 Oxford Avenue. Gold's grave is in Section O, six rows back from the sign, at GPS 40.03980, -75.08570.

In 1953, Julius and Ethel Rosenberg were famously executed for selling atomic-bomb secrets to the Soviet Union. But the man who facilitated their treachery was Harry Gold (1910–1972), the courier who carried the plans from Manhattan Project scientist Klaus Fuchs to David Greenglass, who passed them on to Julius.

Grave of courier Harry Gold, who was involved in the Rosenbergs' spying conspiracy. Strangely, the year of birth is incorrect. It is actually 1910.

Greenglass was Ethel's brother and was probably guiltier in the conspiracy than she was. He saved himself from the Rosenbergs' fate by testifying against and condemning his own sister. He was joined in this damning testimony by Gold, who was also spared the death penalty.

Gold was sentenced to thirty years in prison but released in 1965. He died in 1972 at age sixty-one.

GARY HEIDNIK'S HOUSE OF HORRORS
Kensington

The original house has been torn down, but a nearly identical one has been built at 3520 North Marshall Street, or GPS 40.00521, -75.14030. This is private property.

Gary Heidnik was a strange dude, living in a filthy slum even though he was worth $500,000 and owned a Rolls-Royce. The hallways of his house were papered with coins and dollar bills, taped from one end to the other. The neighborhood was known as the "O.K. Corral" because of a drug-related shootout in the middle of the street.

Heidnik claimed to be a minister to the poor, but he was really a psychopath who abducted six black or Hispanic women and imprisoned them in chains inside his basement. Keeping them naked from the waist down, he subjected them to daily rapes, hoping to father his own "master race." Any perceived infraction caused severe punishment, including starvation, beatings, and screwdrivers shoved into their ears.

On November 26, 1986, he snatched his first victim, a streetwise hooker named Josefina Rivera, from the corner of 3rd and Girard Streets. Back home he handcuffed her and marched her into the basement, where he secured her to a bare mattress with a chain.

Three days later Heidnik abducted Sandra Lindsay, a mildly mentally disabled woman he'd known for four years. When she disappeared her family suspected Heidnik and called police. But the cop who talked to Heidnik never went inside the house and didn't check his police record, which included a previous arrest and conviction for abducting and raping a different mentally disabled woman.

A month after Lindsay, Lisa Thomas was added to the group, and, a week later, Debra Dudley. Number five, Jacqueline Askins, was brought in two weeks later.

Because of Lindsay's mental disability, she wasn't able to comprehend all of Heidnik's commands and subsequently was singled out for days of punishment. On February 7, 1987, after a week of hanging by one wrist from a water-pipe, she became feverish and vomited. When she finally passed out, Heidnik uncuffed her. Believing she was faking, he kicked her into the dirt pit he'd dug in the basement floor, where she soon died.

He dismembered her, putting some of her body parts in his freezer and cooking others. He then mixed the cooked body parts with dog food and fed the foul concoction to the other captive women.

Rivera, realizing that she might end up the same way, began worming her way into Heidnik's good graces. In return he gave her special privileges and dismissed her from the punishment he dealt to the others.

On March 18, 1987, Heidnik decided that Dudley, Thomas, and Askins needed extraordinary discipline and ordered them into the pit, which he had filled with water. Bringing a plugged-in frayed extension cord over to them, he touched it to the nearest chain. Screaming in pain, Dudley was electrocuted and died; Heidnik later dumped her body in New Jersey.

Since he'd lost two sex-slaves, Heidnik snatched Agnes Adams on March 23, 1987, and added her to his basement hell-hole.

The next day Rivera persuaded Heidnik to let her have a short visit with her family. She promised to return at midnight and meet him at the corner of Sixth and Girard Streets. When he dropped her off, she went straight to the police, who didn't believe her story at first. Nevertheless Heidnik was arrested that night on the corner where he was to meet Rivera.

Heidnik was convicted and sentenced to death. He was executed on July 6, 1999. He is buried at Holy Sepulchre Cemetery, Section P, 4001 West Cheltenham Avenue in Cheltenham, at GPS 40.08677, -75.17223.

MARIE NOE'S DEAD BABIES
Kensington

The Noes lived in several homes, all within a few blocks of each other, at 240 West Atlantic Street (GPS 40.00417, -75.13353), 3452 North Rosehill Street (GPS 40.00212, -75.12351), 3447 North American Street (GPS 40.00336, -75.13380), and 3451 North American Street (GPS 40.00343, -75.13381). This is private property.

Starting in 1949, Marie Noe murdered more of her own children than any mother in American history. Eight babies came and went in the space of nineteen years. She was unable to tolerate their crying and suffocated them all. Only one made it past her first birthday. Two other babies died of natural causes in the hospital shortly after birth.

At first Marie's baby woes were attributed to crib-death, and they garnered the sympathy of her neighbors and medical professionals, and even *LIFE* magazine. But, with each successive demise—some within mere days or weeks of going home with Marie—suspicions were raised. Doctors did every test they could think of on the infants, but they all appeared to be healthy. With no proof of murder but with absolute dread, neo-natal nurses watched each child leave with the Noes. They tearfully predicted the next time they'd see the infant, it'd be dead. They were never wrong.

Each time Marie rushed a child to the hospital or called for an ambulance, she claimed the baby had turned blue and stopped breathing. The first four children—Richard, one month; Elizabeth, five months; Jacqueline, three weeks; and Arthur Jr., five days—were buried at Greenwood Cemetery, Adams Avenue and Arrott Street. There's a small headstone for both Richard and Elizabeth at GPS 40.02169, -75.09531.

The last four—Constance, one month; Mary Lee, six months; Catherine, one year and two months; and Arthur Joseph, five months—rest at New Cathedral Cemetery, North Front and East Luzerne Streets. (The cemetery is bisected by Front St.) Mary Lee is buried in the western part of the cemetery at GPS 40.00815, -75.12927. Catherine and Arthur Joseph are next to each other, covered by a two-person in-ground marker in the eastern part, in Section K, near the road, at GPS 40.00973, -75.12494. The office won't divulge where Constance is buried.

Marie got away with the slayings for thirty years, until the cases of two other baby-murdering moms—Waneta Hoyt and Marybeth Tinning—caught the attention of reporters and authorities in Philadelphia. As they looked through old cases of multiple SIDS deaths in the city, Marie's case stood out.

On March 15, 1998, the police questioned seventy-year-old Marie and her unsuspecting husband, Arthur. Within minutes Marie was confessing to cops in a calm, detached manner the real details of the children's deaths.

Marie was sentenced to twenty years of house arrest. Wearing an ankle bracelet, she's unable to leave the house except for doctor appointments. Although devastated when he found out the truth about his kids' deaths, Arthur stuck by Marie's side until he died in 2009.

THE LETHAL SHOEMAKER
Kensington

Kallinger's former home and shop is at the southeast corner of North Front and East Sterner Streets, or GPS 39.99135, -75.13072. This is private property.

By all reports, Joseph Kallinger was a very good shoemaker. As a father . . . not so much. He was a schizophrenic who talked to "God" and believed the Lord was ordering him to kill people. He had a secret hideaway where he would sit in a deep pit and chant for hours at a time. It was also where he received his murder instructions from Heaven.

Kallinger enlisted the aid of his thirteen-year-old son Michael in his crimes. The pair's first victim was Jose Collazo, a young teenager they picked up on July 7, 1974, at the Mann Recreation Center, North 5th Street and Allegheny Avenue (GPS 40.00056, -75.13829). With the promise of money to help them move boxes of ribbon, Jose accompanied them to an abandoned rug factory, where he was killed and castrated. Kallinger took the youngster's genitals home with him and kept them in his shop for days.

The shoemaker then got the "heavenly" message that his sixteen-year-old son, Joey, was next on God's list, so he and Mike tried twice to kill him before finally succeeding on July 28, 1974, at a construction site (now "The Gallery" shopping mall) at Ninth and Market Streets in Center City (GPS 39.95147, -75.15527). At night, after the workmen had gone, Joseph, Mike, and Joey climbed down the stairs of a partially demolished building to a stagnant pool of water at the bottom. His father and brother tied Joey to a ladder, and then tipped it over into the pool, so the teenager would hit the water face-down. He struggled to breathe and begged them to help him, but they watched his death-throes impassively, and then went home. Joey is buried at Whitemarsh Memorial Park, 1169 Limekiln Pike, Ambler, Section H, Lot 3163, or GPS 40.21870, -75.19296.

The Kallingers' final slaying happened during a home invasion in New Jersey on January 8, 1975. Maria Fasching was stabbed to death when she showed up unexpectedly during the crime. A bloody shirt Joseph left behind contained a laundry mark. Tracing it to Kallinger, the police arrested him and Michael. Joseph received life in prison for the murders, and Mike went into foster care. Kallinger died in prison on March 26, 1996, when he choked on his own vomit in the infirmary. His burial spot is unknown.

RABBLE-ROUSER LEWIS LEVIN
Kensington

The site of the inferno is the west side of Cadwallader Street, from Jefferson Street to Master Street, or GPS 39.97375, -75.14082.

The Know-Nothing Party was the catch-all moniker for several secret political organizations that had sprung up around the country in the mid-1800s in virulent opposition to America's open immigration policy. Their biggest target was Irish-Catholics, who were pouring into the US in massive numbers as they fled staggering unemployment and starvation in their native land. When asked, members would reply, "I know nothing."

These groups aimed to bar Irish-Catholics and other immigrants from voting or obtaining political office, and they advocated a twenty-one-year waiting period for foreigners to attain citizenship. Their rolls grew quickly.

When Bishop Francis Kenrick of Philadelphia petitioned the local school board to allow Catholic schoolchildren to use the Catholic Bible for morning prayers in the public schools instead of the standard-issue Protestant King James version, the Know-Nothings erupted in protest. Falsely accusing the Catholics of trying to remove the holy book from the schools, party members called for demonstrations around the city. The largest of these, attracting about four thousand people, was held at Independence Hall (of all places).

Among the speakers rousing the crowds was Lewis C. Levin, a newspaper editor whose two papers carried daily diatribes against Irish-Catholic power. Over a three-day period, from May 6 to 8, 1844, howling mobs descended on the Irish enclave of Kensington and burned, looted, and shot at everything in their path. An entire city block of row-houses was set on fire, and two Catholic churches—St. Michael's at 1445 North 2nd Street (GPS 39.97334, -75.13862) and St. Augustine's at 4th and Vine Streets (GPS 39.95546, -75.14601)— were burned to the ground. (They've since been rebuilt. In front of St. Augustine's is an information kiosk about the riots.) Twenty-nine Irish homes were destroyed, fourteen people were killed, and fifty more were injured before the state militia restored order. Even Mayor John Scott was stoned when he tried to stop the crowd from burning St. Augustine's.

Levin was arrested and charged with "exciting [sic] to riot and treason." He was merely ordered to pay a small fine.

In spite of the riots (or maybe because of them), Levin was elected to Congress three times. But after his third term, he was accused of bribing members of the Pennsylvania General Assembly to choose him as the next US Senator from Pennsylvania. He was never charged, but his political career was over.

He soon suffered a mental breakdown and was admitted to the Philadelphia Hospital for the Insane at 111 North 49th Street (GPS 39.96101, -75.21816). The old building is still standing and has been designated a National Historic Landmark. Levin died there on March 14, 1860, and was buried in Laurel Hill Cemetery in North Philadelphia. His grave is in Section 10, Lot 32, or GPS 39.99842, -75.18862. Ironically, his wife and daughter both converted to Catholicism after his death.

See also "Laurel Hill Cemetery" (North Philadelphia).

BIRTHPLACE OF MOBSTER "LEGS" DIAMOND
Kensington

Diamond's former house is at 2350 East Albert Street, or GPS 39.98150, -75.11982. This is private property.

Jack "Legs" Diamond was a gangster born here on July 10, 1897. An associate of gambler Arnold Rothstein, who allegedly fixed the 1919 World Series, most of Diamond's criminal activities took place in New York. He was arrested more than two dozen times and escaped four assassination attempts. No other gangster survived as many bullets as he did, and the other mobsters called him "The Clay Pigeon of the Underworld." He proudly boasted, "They haven't invented the bullet that could kill me." But, oh, yes, they had. On December 17, 1931, he was shot three times in the head as he slept off a drunk in Albany.

Diamond is buried in Mount Olivet Cemetery in Maspeth, New York.

THE MAINLINE MURDERS
King of Prussia

The presumed murder site, the former Smith house, is at 705 West Valley Forge Road, or GPS 40.10374, -75.39783. This is private property.

Susan Reinert, a "Plain Jane" divorced mother of two, couldn't believe her luck when a charming, bright man named William Bradfield wooed her and proposed marriage in the late 1970s. They both taught English at Upper Merion High School, 435 Crossfield Road in King of Prussia (GPS 40.09643, -75.37830). Located in the prestigious, wealthy area known as the "Mainline," the school was considered one of the best in the state.

Even though she knew Bradfield had been living with another female teacher for the past fifteen years, Susan accepted his proposal. Caught up in his charismatic thrall, she changed her will,

Susan Reinert and her children were last seen alive in front of her home.

leaving everything to him, and made him the beneficiary of her substantial life insurance policies. She also gave him a tidy inheritance from her mother to "invest."

With Reinert's money almost his, Bradfield began telling three colleagues that he believed the school principal, Dr. Jay C. Smith—a bizarre man students and teachers had nicknamed "The Prince of Darkness"—was planning to kill Reinert. Swearing them to secrecy, he persuaded the male teachers to join him on several late-night stake-outs at Reinert's house to "protect her," and had them monitor Smith's activities. None of his colleagues ever questioned his actions, thought to notify Susan of his murder theory, or called the police.

During this time Principal Smith was already in trouble with the law. He was accused of robbing two Sears stores and weapons violations. And police were investigating the suspicious disappearances of Smith's daughter Stephanie and her husband, Eddie Hunsberger, who were both financial drains on Smith. The two heroin addicts vanished in 1978 and have never been found.

Then things got weirder. On the evening of June 22, 1979, in the middle of a freak hailstorm, Reinert's next-door neighbor heard the phone ringing in Susan's house at 662 Woodcrest Avenue in Ardmore (GPS 39.99946, -75.30146), then watched in amazement as Susan, despite the weather, herded her children, Karen, eleven, and Michael, ten, into her car and drove away.

That same night, Bradfield's colleagues waited for him to take them on a planned trip to Cape May, New Jersey, but he didn't arrive until after 11 p.m. Nervous and disheveled, he hurried them out the door and into the car. Halfway to the shore, Bradfield suddenly announced he believed this was going to be the weekend that Jay Smith would kill Reinert.

A few days later Smith was sentenced in Harrisburg for the burglaries and gun crimes—almost at the same time that an anonymous tip led police to Susan Reinert's naked, battered body in the back of her Plymouth hatchback in the parking lot of the Host Inn (now Holiday Inn), 148 Sheridan Drive, in the Harrisburg suburb of New Cumberland (GPS 40.24234, -76.80038). Her two children were missing. Under Reinert's body investigators found a comb imprinted with the name of Smith's Army Reserve unit. An autopsy revealed she'd been savagely beaten, then injected with a fatal dose of morphine.

From his jail cell Smith wrote an urgent letter to his dying wife to clean his car *thoroughly* and get rid of the carpet in the basement. A police search of Smith's car revealed a small clasp pin with a "P" on it from the Philadelphia Museum of Art, where Karen Reinert had gone on a school field trip. She loved the pin and wore it all the time, long after the trip was over. And a search of Smith's now rugless basement uncovered a hair matching Susan's. Also, Smith's previous robbery investigation file contained pictures of chains in his basement similar to the ones that had made marks on Susan's body.

As the evidence against Smith accumulated, the three other teachers finally told police their strange tale of Bradfield's activities. Now police believed that Bradfield and Smith had conspired to kill Reinert and share her wealth. They theorized that Bradfield had tricked Reinert into meeting Smith, and that the principal had killed her and her children inside his house. Bradfield then dumped the children's bodies, causing him to be late for the Jersey trip, while Smith drove their mother's corpse to Harrisburg, where he was to appear for his court case.

At Bradfield's murder trial the prosecutor made a point that only Susan's body was found, because the insurance and estate would only be paid to Bradfield if there was proof of her death. The children were worth nothing to him, the prosecutor surmised, so their bodies were hidden elsewhere. Bradfield was convicted of three counts of murder and received a life sentence.

With the help of jailhouse snitches to whom the principal had allegedly confessed, Smith was also convicted and received the death penalty. But Smith appealed his conviction, declaring that Bradfield had framed him. The Pennsylvania Supreme Court granted his appeal and set him free, citing egregious prosecutorial misconduct (suppressing potentially exculpatory evidence) that had rendered his conviction null and void. They also refused to allow a re-trial.

Bradfield died of a heart attack while in prison on January 16, 1998. He took the whereabouts of the Reinert children to his grave. But, in his cell, authorities found a photograph of a triangular rock that appeared to have been taken in the woods (and police speculated that it showed the mysterious spot where he buried the children's bodies). Bradfield was buried at Hopewell United Methodist Church Cemetery, 852 Hopewell Road, Downingtown. The grave is in the South Yard, third row, at GPS 40.03727, -75.73499.

Smith died in 2009, proclaiming his innocence to the end. He's buried at Chapel Lawn Memorial Park, Memorial Highway (Route 415) and Country Club Road, Dallas. His unmarked grave is in the Veteran's Section, Lot 314, Space 6, or GPS 41.34479, -75.99735.

The definitive book on the case, *Echoes in the Darkness,* by Joseph Wambaugh was turned into a mini-series of the same name.

THE ABDUCTION OF AIMEE WILLARD
Media

The I-476 South, Exit 3/Route 1 off-ramp is at GPS 39.93691, -75.36694. A large wooden flower with "Aimee" on it stands at the spot, along with teddy bears and other memorial trinkets hanging from an evergreen tree.

On June 20, 1996, local lacrosse star Aimee Willard enjoyed a night out with friends at Smokey Joe's in Wayne, before heading home in her car at about 2 a.m. The bright and bubbly twenty-two-year-old had no idea a predator named Arthur Bomar was following her.

As she took exit 3 from the Blue Route (I-476), she was bumped from the back by Bomar's car so she pulled to the shoulder to check the damage. Pulling up behind her, Bomar got out and hit her with a tire iron, then dragged her into his car and drove away. Her empty car, the engine still running, was found a few minutes later by an ambulance crew.

The following afternoon, Aimee's nude body, raped and battered, was discovered on a trash-strewn vacant lot at 16th Street and Indiana Avenue, in North Philadelphia (GPS 39.99894, -75.15679). Her murder went unsolved for a year until Bomar was arrested driving a car belonging to missing woman Maria Cabuenos, who hadn't been seen for three months. His DNA matched evidence on Aimee.

The search for Maria ended sadly almost two years later on January 1, 1998, when her skeletal remains were found in dense woods in Bucks County. Like Aimee, she had suffered a severe blow to the back of her head. Bomar was convicted and awaits execution.

When Aimee's mother discovered that Bomar had been released early from a Nevada prison and, despite three arrests in Pennsylvania, had never had his parole revoked, she worked tirelessly for a new federal law to keep dangerous felons incarcerated longer. Known as "Aimee's Law," it was passed by Congress and signed by President Clinton in 2000.

SUMMER LEADS TO A FALL
Merion

The former Rabinowitz home is at 526 Winding Way, or GPS 40.01362, -75.24629. This is private property.

While his attractive wife, Stefanie, worked as a lawyer, Craig Rabinowitz claimed to own a business that imported surgical gloves from Asia. In fact the enterprise didn't exist. Instead Rabinowitz spent nearly every day at a strip club called Delilah's Den, 100 Spring Garden Street in Philadelphia (GPS 39.95960, -75.13962), running up a huge tab of $3,000 a week.

He'd become infatuated with a dancer there, Shannon Reinert, whose stage name was "Summer." To shower her with goodies, he borrowed money from his friends and relatives as "investments" in his fake company. He even used some of his wife's stock portfolio to buy gifts and furniture for his crush.

As debts mounted and his "investors" began asking for their money back, Rabinowitz knew he needed quick cash. He took out two life insurance policies, totaling $1.5 million, on his unsuspecting wife, and then waited for the right moment.

On April 29, 1997, he sprang into action. Slipping sleeping pills into his wife's nightcap, he watched her pass out, and then carried her upstairs to the bathtub. He lowered Stefanie into the water, holding her head below the surface. Revived, she struggled mightily, so Craig strangled her instead. He later called paramedics, faking hysterical grief as they performed CPR. Stefanie was pronounced dead at Lankenau Hospital.

His efforts to quickly bury his wife were thwarted when a suspicious coroner ordered a thorough autopsy that revealed the tell-tale marks of strangulation.

While Stefanie's parents and friends mourned, Craig visited Summer and planned their future. Armed with a warrant, police found a piece of paper hidden in the attic on which Craig had listed his considerable debts and the amount he expected to collect on Stefanie's insurance policies. Subtracting the debt from the insurance pay-out, he'd callously calculated the total that would be left for him and Summer.

Charged with murder, Craig pleaded guilty and was sentenced to life in prison.

Stefanie is buried under her maiden name, Newman, at Mount Lebanon Cemetery, 1200 Bartram Avenue in Collingdale. Her grave is in Section 19, Lot 19, Grave 2, or GPS 39.91103, -75.28681.

MURDER AT THE GENERAL WAYNE INN
Merion Station

The General Wayne Inn is at 625 Montgomery Avenue, or GPS 40.00910, -75.25338.

Established in 1704, this colonial-era tavern has hosted the likes of General "Mad" Anthony Wayne, George Washington, the Marquis de Lafayette, and Edgar Allan Poe. It's even reputed to be haunted. But a modern-day dispute between business partners would add a new ghost to the mix.

Best friends James Webb and Guy Sileo owned the inn together but disagreed about what to do when the business faltered. Webb wanted to sell it to stem the hemorrhage of money; Sileo wanted to ride out the bad times. The two men argued about it daily.

On December 26, 1996, Sileo crept up to Webb's office on the third floor of the pub and shot him to death. He hoped the police would blame the crime on a robber, and he would receive the hefty insurance money the partners carried on each other, enough to keep the bar afloat for some time. But the cops quickly zeroed in on their suspect, and Sileo was arrested. He received a life sentence at his trial.

Since then two more owners have failed to make a go of the inn. It was eventually sold to the congregation of a local synagogue, which renovated it and opened it as the Chabad Center for Jewish Life. Happily, they retained the outside appearance of the historic inn.

James Webb (1965–1996) is buried in Mount Hope Cemetery, 4022 Concord Road, Aston, at GPS 39.87157, -75.44114.

The historic General Wayne Inn was the scene of a modern murder.

GENERAL WINFIELD SCOTT HANCOCK'S GRAVE
Norristown

Montgomery Cemetery is at 1 Hartranft Avenue, near Jackson Street. Hancock is buried in a small fenced-in mausoleum to the far left of the entrance, or GPS 40.11940, -75.36282.

Named after War of 1812 hero General Winfield Scott, Hancock (1824–1886) also became a general and a war hero, distinguishing himself in the Civil War, especially during the Battle of Gettysburg, where he commanded the Union troops who repulsed Pickett's Charge. Although he was wounded in the battle, he refused to leave the field until the battle was won.

After Lincoln's assassination Hancock presided over the executions of the condemned conspirators—George Atzerodt, David Herold, Lewis Payne (aka Powell), and Mary Surratt. On July 7, 1865, before the scheduled hangings, Mary's lawyers obtained a writ of habeas corpus for her and served it on General Hancock. He was to produce her at 10 a.m.

Hancock informed President Andrew Johnson of the writ, and Johnson immediately voided it. In court Hancock told the judge the order had been vacated by presidential decree. The executions went off uninterrupted, with the four co-conspirators hanged simultaneously inside the Old Arsenal Penitentiary in Washington, DC at GPS 38.866644, -77.017195.

In 1880, General Hancock was the Democratic presidential nominee, but was defeated by Republican James Garfield, who, like Lincoln, was assassinated. In 1886, Hancock died of an infected carbuncle at age sixty-one while still commanding the Military Division of the Atlantic.

For more sites related to the Lincoln assassination, see *The Crime Buff's Guide to Outlaw Washington, DC* (Globe Pequot Press, 2012).

LAUREL HILL CEMETERY
North Philadelphia
Laurel Hill is at 3822 Ridge Avenue, or GPS 40.00415, -75.18749.

Laurel Hill Cemetery was founded in 1836 and contains many famous people, including General George Meade, who won the Battle of Gettysburg, and six passengers from the *Titanic*. But it also has some crime-history figures, including:

- **Henry Deringer** (1786–1868) invented the tiny one- or two-shot pistol that could easily be concealed in a pocket. One of Deringer's pistols was used by John Wilkes Booth to assassinate Abraham Lincoln. A reporter erroneously spelled Deringer's pistol with two Rs in one of his stories, and the spelling stuck. The gun is called a Derringer to this day. The gunmaker's tall obelisk is in the Shrubbery Section, Lots 10-14, or GPS 40.00406, -75.18858.

- **Lewis C. Levin** (1808–1860) incited the anti-Irish riots in Philadelphia that took fourteen lives. His grave is in Section 10, Lot 32, or GPS 39.99841, -75.18865. See "Rabble-Rouser Lewis Levin" (Kensington).

TED BUNDY'S CHILDHOOD HOME
Roxborough
Samuel Cowell's former home and garden nursery business was at 7202 Ridge Road, or GPS 40.04537, -75.23237. A pizza parlor now stands on the site.

Most crime buffs associate infamous serial killer Ted Bundy with Seattle, Utah, Colorado, or Florida. But Bundy spent his first four years in Philadelphia at the home of his grandparents, Samuel and Eleanore

College student Ted Bundy lived in this house in 1969.

Cowell. Born illegitimate in a home for unwed girls, Bundy grew up believing his teenage mother, Louise Cowell, was actually his sister, until he learned the truth as a young man. Just how much this revelation led to his future sociopathic behavior is ripe for speculation.

Even as a small child, he exhibited some unsettling behavior— arranging an entire set of kitchen knives around the body of his sleeping aunt and sneaking into the nursery greenhouse to ogle his grandfather's pornography.

In 1969, Bundy returned to Philadelphia and briefly attended Temple University while staying at his grandfather's new home at 4039 South Warner Street, Lafayette Hill (GPS 40.09353, -75.25493). During this time, two co-eds were abducted together and murdered at the Jersey Shore, just one hour away. The crime has never been solved, giving rise to speculation that Bundy's killing career may have begun five years earlier than previously thought. He hinted his guilt to his prison psychologist.

Shortly before Bundy was executed in Florida in 1989, he confessed to thirty murders, although investigators believe it could be many more. After his electrocution the serial killer's ashes were reportedly scattered over Washington state's Cascade Range.

A DEADLY BASEBALL BRAWL
South Philadelphia

McFadden's Restaurant and Saloon (Ballpark) is at 1 Citizens Bank Way (11th and Pattison Streets), or GPS 39.90483, -75.16750.

Philadelphia sports fans are notoriously rowdy. But on July 25, 2009, the unruliness turned deadly when about thirty drunken fans left a Fishtown tavern to attend a Phillies game at Citizens Bank Park. By the second inning, they began tussling with a bachelor-party group of eight whose seats they were trying to steal. Things got ugly and the Fishtown bunch was ejected from the stadium, so they drowned their sorrows at the nearby McFadden's. After the sixth inning the bachelor-party celebrants also showed up in the crowded bar, and the trash talk ramped up again.

David Sale, twenty-two-year-old brother of the bride-to-be, deliberately doused one of the antagonists with beer. A fistfight erupted and both groups were tossed out of the bar, but the brawl merely spilled into the surrounding parking lots. On Parking Lot M, outside Jetro's Food Warehouse (GPS 39.90346, -75.16363), the rumble became murderous.

Three of the Fishtown gang took turns beating, kicking, and stomping Sale. As he lay helpless, one of them teed up his head like a football and viciously kicked it, killing him.

The three assailants eventually pleaded guilty to involuntary manslaughter; the longest sentence was nine to eighteen years in prison.

Sale was buried at Grandview Cemetery in Johnstown.

NOT-SO-GENTLE DEATH OF A DON
South Philadelphia

The former Bruno home is at 934 Snyder Avenue, or GPS 39.92337, -75.16243. This is private property.

Italian-born Angelo Bruno was called "The Gentle Don" because he didn't kill quite as many people as the other mob bosses. He ruled the Philly crime-family from 1959 until 1980, longer than any other boss. But all good things come to an end.

On March 21, 1980, his chauffeur drove him home from a fine Italian dinner. As he parked in front of the house, a hidden assassin sprang out of the shadows and blasted Bruno in the back of the head with a shotgun.

Mob boss Angelo Bruno was assassinated in front of his house.

The hit was allegedly ordered by Antonio "Tony Bananas" Capo-nigro, Bruno's *consigliere*. If so, Caponigro didn't have long to savor his coup. A month later he was found stuffed into a body bag in the trunk of a car in New York with $300 jammed into his mouth and anus, signifying greed.

Bruno (1910–1980) was buried in Holy Cross Cemetery in Yeadon; his grave is in Section 23, Row 2, Plot 16, or GPS 39.93237, -75.25663.

See also "Holy Cross Cemetery" (Yeadon).

CHICKEN TAKE-OUT
South Philadelphia

The former Testa home is at 2117 Porter Street, or GPS 39.92106, -75.18303. This is private property.

Philip "Chicken Man" Testa took over the Philly mob after the murder of Angelo Bruno, but if he hoped to have as long a run as the former boss, he'd be sadly disappointed.

Grave of mob boss Philip "Chicken Man" Testa

One year later, on March 15, 1981, he was blown up by a bomb planted under his porch. The killers were reputed to be Frank Narducci and Rocco Marinucci. But police couldn't question them because the two gangsters themselves were soon also rubbed out, allegedly by goons of the new boss, Nicodemo "Little Nicky" Scarfo. Scarfo would never be called a "gentle don." Over two dozen mobsters would be eliminated after his takeover.

Bruce Springsteen's song "Atlantic City" refers to Testa's gruesome death, although he incorrectly sings that Testa's house was also destroyed. It wasn't. Only the porch took the hit, and it was repaired beautifully. Today the house and porch look exactly the same as they did when Testa lived there.

Testa (1924–1981) was buried at Holy Cross Cemetery in Yeadon, not far from Anthony Bruno. His grave is in Section 21, Row 3, Plot 29, or GPS 39.93145, -75.25564.

See also "Holy Cross Cemetery" (Yeadon).

THE MUMMERS RAID
South Philadelphia
The Downtowners Fancy Brigade Club is at 148–150 Snyder Avenue, or GPS 39.92176, -75.14972.

The Mummers are feather-and-sequin-clad musicians who have famously strutted their stuff down Broad Street on New Year's Day for over one hundred years. The group has always prided itself on its family-friendly entertainment. But when the police raided the group's Downtowners Club on October 11, 2011, they found strutting of another kind going on. And family-friendly it was *not*!

A full-fledged orgy of prostitution, boozing, and drugs was happening. Wearing little to nothing, hookers were openly plying their trade in front of about seventy partiers, while two prominent Mummers served hard drinks at the bar without a liquor license.

Ten women made the mistake of trying to solicit the cops and were promptly arrested, along with their pimp and the two bartenders.

Shocked and embarrassed, leaders of the Mummers Association disavowed all knowledge of the "festivities" that had been going on in the club for months and quickly moved to suspend their two errant colleagues.

THE FIRST WARD HORROR
South Philadelphia

The former site of the Deering farm is now a food distribution center at 3301 South Galloway Street, or GPS 39.90748, -75.15538.

German immigrant Anton Probst came to America in 1863 to seek his fortune, but unlike most of his fellow countrymen, he didn't want to work for it.

Probst made a living by enlisting in the Union Army during the Civil War, pocketing his $300 bonus, then deserting, only to turn up in different places where he'd repeat his scam several times. When the war ended, Probst found himself broke and desperate.

He hired on at the Philadelphia-area farm owned by Christopher Deering, who lived there with his wife Julia and their children, William, John, Thomas, Anna, and baby Emily. Probst's co-worker was Cornelius Carey, a friendly, industrious teenager.

It didn't take long for Probst's laziness to become evident to the Deerings. And when he started leering and making crude remarks to Julia, she demanded that her husband fire him. Out of work, Probst faked an illness and was taken in by a charity hospital, but his malingering soon wore out his welcome there, too.

Hat in hand, Probst returned to the Deering farm and begged for his job back. The soft-hearted Christopher relented and hired him again, but Probst was already hatching a monstrous scheme. And on April 7, 1866, he saw his chance.

That morning Christopher took his carriage to the train station to pick up his niece, Elizabeth Dolan, who was coming for a visit. The rest of the family stayed home, except son William, who was away at his grandparents' house.

Probst and Carey were working together in the fields when they took a break under a tree. As soon as the boy's back was turned, Probst cleaved his head with an axe, killing him instantly.

After dumping Carey's body in a haystack, Probst went to the house and lured Julia out to the barn, where he also crushed her head with the axe. Dragging her body into a horse stall, he covered it with straw and returned to the farmhouse. One by one, he led each child to the barn under the pretense that their mother wanted to see them. When they got there they were quickly dispatched and hidden with their mother under the straw.

Probst then waited for Christopher and his niece to return. When the carriage drove up, Probst led Christopher into the barn, while Elizabeth went to the house to freshen up. Probst killed him there.

Finally he brought Elizabeth to the deadly barn and killed her, too. He spent the rest of the day ransacking the house for valuables, scoring a mere $13 and a pocket-watch. After pawning the watch he drank away his miserable fortune at a local tavern.

When the bodies were discovered, the police searched the city and soon found the drunken errant field-hand. He was convicted of the eight murders and sentenced to die.

After his hanging, Probst's body was donated to Jefferson Medical Center, where his skeleton was displayed for several years before being discarded. The Deerings' mutilated bodies were also displayed at the local funeral home, with the greedy funeral director charging $10 a head to peek at them. Despite $10 being a month's salary at the time, thousands came to gawk.

The family was finally buried at St. Mary's Cemetery at 10th and Moore Streets, but even then they weren't allowed to rest in peace. When the space was needed for construction of St. Maria Goretti High School in the 1950s, all the bodies in the graveyard were dug up and re-interred in a mass grave in Holy Cross Cemetery. Their mass grave is below the large marble marker with a statue of the Virgin Mary in Section 14, at GPS 39.92635, -75.25758. See "Holy Cross Cemetery" (Yeadon).

Strangely enough, fifty years later, on November 17, 1916, tragedy struck the Deering family again. Mary Deering, the widow of lone-survivor William Deering, was also murdered by a robber inside her home at 51 North 51st Street, West Philadelphia (GPS 39.96095, -75.22255).

FATHER DIVINE
South Philadelphia

The Circle Mission Church is at 764–772 South Broad Street, or GPS 39.94111, -75.16629.

His real name was reportedly George Baker, but he preferred his made-up one—Father Major Jealous Divine. Considered to be America's first cult leader, Divine was a black, self-made preacher, and his charismatic style brought dozens of people to hear him speak. Telling followers he was God, Divine attracted a bevy of female acolytes whose husbands had him arrested for "lunacy."

At court he refused to give his name and was tried as "John Doe, Alias God." Acquitted, he took his flock to Brooklyn, New York, where they formed a commune in an apartment building. He forbade them to smoke, drink, gamble, or engage in sex—even if married. And, of course, everything they owned was to be given to him.

In 1919, he moved his growing, predominantly black congregation to affluent Long Island, New York, where horrified white neighbors had Divine and his flock arrested for disturbing the peace. The incident was reported luridly in the New York City tabloids, making Father Divine an instant celebrity and earning him a host of new

Father Divine's impressive mansion, "Woodmont," was a gift from a parishioner.

supporters. The group now named itself "The International Peace Mission Movement."

At Divine's trial dyspeptic Judge Lewis Smith called Divine a fraud and "a menace to society," and sentenced him to a year in prison and a $500 fine. Two weeks later, after the judge died of a massive heart attack, Divine remarked demurely, "I hated to do it."

His church soon expanded across the United States, then the world, with estimates of up to two million adherents. And the money flowed in. The movement relocated to Philadelphia, where it remains today. A wealthy follower named, appropriately, John Devoute, gave Divine his beautiful French Gothic mansion, Woodmont, at 1622 Spring Mill Road in Gladwynne (GPS 40.06378, -75.29077). It's open for tours, but be prepared to hear a religious spiel.

In fairness, Father Divine did some good with his money, too. In 1948, he bought a luxury high-rise apartment building at 699 North Broad Street (GPS 39.96676, -75.16036). Calling it the "Divine Lorraine," he turned it into the first racially integrated hotel in the US. The first floor was opened as a public dining area, where low-cost meals could be purchased by the poor. His church sold it in 2000 to a developer, who was supposed to turn it into condos, but nothing has happened, and it's becoming a derelict wreck. There's a historical marker in front that tells about it and Divine.

With his fame spreading, Divine came to the attention of a young Indiana preacher named Jim Jones, who decided to see for himself what all the fuss was about. In 1958, Jones visited Father Divine at Woodmont and listened to his sermons at Circle Mission, which inspired him to start his own church—"The People's Temple." Like Divine, Jones made his devotees call him "Father," and accepted all races into his fold. When Father Divine died on September, 10, 1965, and was buried on the grounds of his palatial estate, Jones claimed that his spirit had entered his body, and that he was now God.

In 1971, Jones and two hundred of his supporters came to Philadelphia and tried to wrest control of Father Divine's empire from Divine's second wife, the young, white Edna Ritchings. But the formidable Edna, who called herself Mrs. S. A. ("Sweet Angel") Divine or "Mother Divine," successfully retained her leadership and runs the church to this day.

Defeated, Jones went on to California and then into criminal infamy in Guyana, leading over nine hundred of his followers into death by suicide in 1978.

GHOST OF THE NATIONAL THEATRE
Southwest Philadelphia

Mount Moriah Cemetery is at South 62nd Street and Kingsessing Avenue. The grave is in Section 149, or GPS 39.934838, -75.240784.

Players at Washington, DC's National Theatre still whisper about the ghost of a murdered actor who legend says was buried in the dirt beneath the modern-day stage. Fact or fable? Well, as Shakespeare's Hamlet said, "The play's the thing."

And the story of ill-fated Shakespearean actor John Edward McCullough has been playing secretly at the National for more than 100 years. The story goes like this:

In the late 1800s, McCullough and a fellow thespian reportedly got into an argument in the theater's basement. Some say it was over an actress, others say it was about a plum role they both wanted.

Either way, shots were fired. McCullough fell dead in that cellar, and his body was hastily buried in the dirt floor—or so the myth goes.

Nobody knew much about McCullough's sudden disappearance, much less his clandestine grave, but people soon began spying McCullough's ghost in the theater, and a legend was born.

In the 1930s, Washington detectives proposed to excavate the dirt floor, but clannish, superstitious theater people revolted, and it never happened. However, when the theater was refurbished in 1984, the legend got new life when a rusty, 1800s pistol was found in the dirt under the stage and donated to the Smithsonian.

Nice story, but McCullough was not murdered. Although one of the most celebrated tragedians of his day, he developed dementia and was committed to an insane asylum in Philadelphia, where he died in 1885 at age fifty-three. He was buried in Mount Moriah under what is said to be the tallest monument ever built to an actor.

MALL SHOOTING SPREE
Springfield

The Springfield Mall is at 1250 Baltimore Pike, or GPS 39.91465, -75.35182.

Although she'd been in a mental hospital fifteen times by age twenty-five, Sylvia Seegrist was still able to purchase a semi-automatic rifle and a thirty-round clip at a gun shop, just by stating on a form that she had no mental problems. Her crazy demeanor was so obvious to the sporting-goods employees at a local K-Mart she'd visited previously that they told her they'd just run out of guns. She even told friends she admired James Huberty, the McDonald's mass-murderer in California, and she copied him by wearing army fatigues constantly, even while working out at the gym.

On October 30, 1985, she got up, dressed in her "camos," and went to the Springfield Mall. She was well-known there for harassing the customers and clerks with her incoherent rantings. She parked her car, reached inside it for her rifle, and began shooting wildly at people in the parking lot.

Hitting nobody, she marched toward the mall itself. Near the Magic Pan restaurant (now a Ruby Tuesday), Seegrist shot two-year-old Recife Cosman dead and injured two other nearby children.

Mumbling to her unseen demons, she burst through the door and purposefully strode through the mall, randomly firing into stores and at the patrons. Dr. Ernest Trout was her next victim. Mortally wounded, he lingered in a coma for a month before dying. More people were hit and injured before Seegrist killed Augustus Ferrara in a walkway.

Thinking the whole episode was a sick Halloween prank and that Seegrist was firing blanks, annoyed grad-student John Laufer grabbed the rifle from her hands as she aimed it at him and informed her that he was taking her to security. Seegrist's spree had lasted only four minutes but left three dead and seven wounded.

Police asked her why she did it. "My family makes me nervous," she replied, as if that explained it perfectly.

She was found guilty but insane and was sentenced to three consecutive life terms. She was the first woman to go on a shooting rampage inside a public place.

MASSACRED BY A MADMAN
Trevose

Roosevelt Memorial Park is at 2701 Old Lincoln Highway. The Cohens' gravesite is in Section Z, at GPS 40.12880, -74.97280.

Howard Unruh was the local oddball in Camden, New Jersey's, quiet neighborhood known as Cramer Hill. A classic quiet loner, he had no job, no friends, and no love life. He was shy about his secret homosexuality, but not of quoting scripture to passersby. He spent his days brooding over imagined slights by his neighbors, keeping a list of each one.

On September 6, 1949, he returned home from a late-night movie to find that someone had broken the wooden gate he'd built in his backyard to keep out the people he resented. Leaving a note for his mother to wake him at 8 a.m., he went to bed to formulate his plan.

When his mother called him at the appointed time, he dressed in a suit, complete with natty bow-tie, and went downstairs to eat breakfast. After threatening his mother with a wrench, causing her to flee, Unruh got his handgun and began a methodical walk through the neighborhood, shooting at everyone he saw.

The Cohen family—pharmacist Maurice, his wife Rose, his mother Minnie, and his young son Charles—owned and lived above the drug store next door to Unruh's apartment. They got on Unruh's list by asking him to stop slamming their metal gate when he cut through their yard. Unruh considered them his enemy, and they didn't much like him either. When they heard the shooting outside, they ran upstairs to hide, but Unruh came in right behind them and shot down all the adults. Only Charles, who hid in a closet, survived the slaughter.

Returning to the street Unruh continued shooting until he ran out of ammunition, then went back to his apartment, which was quickly surrounded by police. Thirteen people died in eleven minutes. Without ever being charged, he was sent to the New Jersey State Hospital in Trenton, where he lived until his death at age eighty-eight in 2009. He was not America's first mass murderer, but with modern media help, he heralded the modern era of mass-shootings.

His young, would-be victim, Charles Cohen, became an advocate for victims and died just six weeks before Unruh. He was buried on the sixtieth anniversary of the rampage at Forest Hills/Shalom Memorial Park, 101 Byberry Road in Huntington Valley. His grave is in Section Gabriel I, Grave 143, or GPS 40.13426, -75.02935.

Unruh (1921–2009) is buried beside his mother in an unmarked grave (GPS 39.945333, -74.345869) at Whiting Memorial Park in Whiting, New Jersey.

For a detailed account of the Unruh shooting spree, see Ron Franscell's 2011 book, *Delivered from Evil.*

A PIECE OF HISTORY
Warminster

The Hartsville Fire Company is at 1195 York Road, or GPS 40.22634, -75.09433.

The worst crime ever perpetrated on American soil was the hijacking of four airplanes by Islamic extremists and the crashing of them into the World Trade Center, the Pentagon, and a Pennsylvania field on September 11, 2001. The horror of this act was seen by millions on television, and the grief is still felt today.

When the little Hartsville Fire Company heard that pieces of the destroyed New York buildings were being distributed around the country, they requested one for a planned memorial they wanted to build in front of the firehouse that would honor the firemen who gave their lives on that terrible day. Their request was granted, and a section of a girder that once held up the mighty towers was donated to them by the New York Port Authority. The fire station asked the community to contribute to the memorial, and an outpouring of cash and volunteer work made the structure a reality.

When the girder arrived in town, it was given a hero's welcome and escorted through the streets by motorcycle cops and fire trucks. The World Trade Center Memorial was dedicated on the

A girder from the destroyed World Trade Center dominates the memorial at the Hartsville Fire Station.

tenth anniversary of the attacks—September 11, 2011. It contains not only the piece of girder, but a scale model of the twin towers and a wall with the names of the brave first-responders who perished that day.

THE EVIL PROFESSOR
Wayne

The former Robb house is at 670 Forest Road, or GPS 40.07319, -75.36888. The house doesn't have a visible house number but is on a rise directly across the street from house number 671. This is private property.

Rafael Robb was not just an Ivy League economics professor. He was also an obsessively controlling husband. Even though he earned $200,000 a year, he demanded that his wife, Ellen, write a monthly check for half the household bills. He belittled her in public and isolated her from her family and friends. After sixteen years of abuse, Ellen told him she was moving out with their daughter. She never got the chance.

On December 22, 2006, Rafael called 911. When the police arrived, they found Ellen on the floor of the kitchen, so viciously beaten they thought she had been shot in the head with a shotgun. The back door window was smashed in, as if there had been a home invasion, but it just didn't look right. When cops learned the marriage had soured, they immediately suspected the professor, who steadfastly denied his guilt for a year. But on the eve of his murder trial, he copped a plea to voluntary manslaughter and was sentenced to five to ten years in prison.

Ellen was buried at Valley Forge Memorial Gardens, 352 South Gulph Road in King of Prussia. Her grave is across the road from a large flagpole and near a marble bench at GPS 40.08193, -75.37361.

THE MOVE FIRE-BOMBING
West Philadelphia
The site of the fire is 6221 Osage Avenue, or GPS 39.95560, -75.24681. This is private property.

A group of dread-locked black activists, all using the last name "Africa" and calling their organization "MOVE," first occupied a house at 307 North 33rd Street (demolished, with a falafel house now at the site at GPS 39.96072, -75.18942). Their confrontational style—obscenity-laced diatribes through loudspeakers at all hours of the day and night and a back-to-nature creed that included dumping garbage and human waste in their yard—didn't exactly endear them to their neighbors. After months of complaints the authorities acted.

On August 8, 1978, no-nonsense Mayor Frank Rizzo, who once declared he would "make Attila the Hun look like a faggot," ordered the police to storm the residence. Under heavy fire from inside they forcibly removed the occupiers. One cop was killed and three others wounded; four firefighters were also injured. MOVE lost that fight, but they weren't about to surrender the war.

Seven years later the radical group took over another house on Osage Avenue. Again, they threw waste in the yard and yelled profane threats at their neighbors. Some of the MOVE members were also wanted for weapons violations.

On May 13, 1985, the police were again outside their door. Despite day-long, bull-horned demands to surrender, the cultists refused to come out and took several pot-shots at the cops. Tear-gas and 10,000 rounds of ammunition were fired into the house to no avail, resulting in a stalemate.

Finally, Wilson Goode, Philadelphia's first black mayor, ordered a police helicopter to drop a "small bomb" on the roof of the house. The bomb caused a raging fire that consumed not only the MOVE house but the entire block of over sixty homes on both sides of the street. Eleven MOVE members, including five children, were killed in the inferno. Only Ramona "Africa" and thirteen-year-old Birdie "Africa" survived. Ramona sued the city and received $500,000 in damages . . . and Philadelphia became known as "The City that Bombed Itself."

SCIENCE PROJECT FROM HELL
West Philadelphia

The former Levin house is at 2447 North 56th Street, or GPS 39.99365, -75.23511. This is private property.

Sixteen-year-old Seymour Levin was a touchy kid. On January 8, 1949, he went to a movie, where he met twelve-year-old Ellis Simons. The two struck up a conversation and discovered they were both interested in scientific experiments, so Seymour invited Ellis to see the fantastic chemistry set he'd received for Christmas.

At the house Levin led Simons to the second-floor bathroom and proudly presented the chemistry set. The younger boy took one look and sniffed, "I have better test tubes at home." Levin was instantly enraged.

After forcibly sodomizing Simons, Levin stabbed him over fifty times, continuing long after the child was dead. He then tied a rope around his body and dragged him downstairs and into the backyard. Levin tried to heave Simons over the hedge into his neighbor's yard, but Simons was too heavy, so Levin simply dumped his body behind the garage.

Cleaning up the blood proved impossible, so when Levin's parents came home, he merely told them his chemistry set had exploded. They bought it . . . at least until the next day when a neighbor found Simons's bloody clothes and called the police.

They found the boy's ravaged body where Levin had left it. After the autopsy, the coroner announced that not one drop of blood remained in Simons's body.

To avoid the death penalty, Levin pleaded guilty and was sent to Eastern Penitentiary. He was paroled twenty-eight years later and he's never been in trouble again. He is believed to be living in New Jersey.

THE GORILLA MAN
West Philadelphia

The murder scene is at 1942 South 60th Street, or GPS 39.932946, -75.230872. It's now a vacant lot.

After a string of slayings on the West Coast in the 1920s, a mysterious killer dubbed "The Gorilla Man" for his brute strength and simian features crossed the country and murdered four people in the Midwest before coming to Philadelphia.

Nearly all of his victims were landladies or women selling their homes. He would look for "Rooms for Rent" or "For Sale" signs and knock on the door, pretending he was interested in living there. If he determined the lady of the house was alone, he'd strangle her, and then usually rape her dead body, often before hiding it under a bed.

By April 27, 1927, fifty-three-year-old Mary McConnell had been trying to sell her house for almost a year, so she welcomed the stranger at her door. Unfortunately he was not interested in her home. He followed her inside, strangled her, and stuffed her body under her bed.

A neighbor at 1935 South 60th Street (GPS 39.93311, -75.23078) saw the man and later described him to the police. The killer tried to attack another Philadelphia woman the next day, but she ran inside and roused her husband. By the time he ran outside, her assailant was gone.

The Gorilla Man continued his trail of death to Buffalo, Detroit, and Chicago, before crossing into Canada, where he murdered two more. His death toll now at twenty-two, he was finally captured in Manitoba.

Identified as Earle Leonard Nelson, a native San Franciscan and former mental patient, he had been released in 1919 from an institution as "improved." Within a year of this "improvement," his murder spree began.

Canadian authorities declined to turn him over to America and, after a trial, hanged him in 1928 at Winnipeg Gaol. Before his death, Nelson was visited in jail by Mary McConnell's husband, William, who asked him why he had killed his wife. Nelson refused to admit his guilt and only told the grieving spouse he hoped the real killer would be found and punished.

Mary and William McConnell are buried together in Arlington Cemetery, 2900 State Road in Drexel Hill. Their graves are in the Lansdowne Section, Lot 164, Grave 6, at GPS 39.95396, -75.29043.

Also at Arlington Cemetery in Drexel Hill:

- **Russell "Dead" Menginie** (1953–1979), outlaw biker, convicted killer, and brother of Anthony "Mangy" Menginie, the former president of the Philadelphia chapter of The

Pagans. During an argument over drugs and stolen goods, Russell shot and wounded Mangy before turning the gun on himself in March 1979. When Mangy later defected to the rival Hells Angels, the two gangs launched bitter open warfare, and Mangy's son, also a Pagan, was assigned to assassinate his own father (but didn't). Russell's grave is in the McKay Section at GPS 39.955872, -75.294664.

HE LAID BOOTH TO REST . . . AND PAID A PRICE
West Philadelphia

Woodlands Cemetery is at 4000 Woodland Avenue. James' grave is in Section N, Lot 353, Grave 1, or GPS 39.94621, -75.20000.

In June 1869, Reverend Fleming James, assistant pastor at St. Luke's Hospital in New York, was visiting a fellow clergyman in Baltimore when his friend was asked to preside over the re-burial of John Wilkes Booth's recently exhumed body. The friend was leaving town, so he asked James to go in his place. James, not considering the ramifications of a Christian blessing for a hated assassin, readily agreed and said a few words of Scripture as Booth's decomposing corpse was lowered into his new tomb in the Booth family plot

The toppled grave marker of Rev. Fleming James

at Green Mount Cemetery, 1501 Greenmount Avenue in Baltimore. John Wilkes Booth's grave is unmarked at his family's request but is among many relatives in the family plot at GPS 39.30706, -76.60606.

When James's enraged bosses found out what he'd done, they fired him. After drifting among churches, he took a job as vicar at All Hallows Episcopal Church, 262 Bent Road in Wyncote (GPS 40.09041, -75.14297). It didn't last long: After just two years James died of a stroke in 1901. But in that time he became so beloved that his congregation dedicated a Tiffany stained-glass window to him above the altar after his death. It remains there to this day.

But old rancor dies hard: James's tombstone has been vandalized and still lies toppled.

DOCTOR OR BUTCHER?
West Philadelphia
The former Women's Medical Society is at 3801 Lancaster Avenue, or GPS 39.960492, -75.197023.

On February 10, 2010, police raided Dr. Kermit Gosnell's clinic, expecting to bust a drug-trafficking operation. Instead, they found horror. Walls and floors were splashed with blood. Moaning, semiconscious women lay on blood-saturated blankets, while unlicensed and unqualified office staff performed procedures. Medical waste was piled in the basement.

Worse, parts of forty-seven aborted fetuses, many of them clearly past the twenty-four-week cutoff mandated by Pennsylvania law, were found in containers. Employees revealed some had been born alive, only to have their spinal cords snipped by the doctor or one of his workers.

Investigators learned one woman had died from a negligent overdose of anesthesia. Probing the clinic's background, authorities discovered that several complaints had been filed with government agencies, but no inspections had been done in seventeen years.

In 2013, Gosnell was convicted of first-degree murder and over 200 other charges. To avoid a possible death sentence, the doctor agreed to life without parole.

HOLY CROSS CEMETERY
Yeadon

Holy Cross is at 626 Baily Road, or GPS 39.93574, -75.25497.

This is the final resting place of some infamous figures in American crime history, including:

- **Herman Webster Mudgett, aka H. H. Holmes** (1861–1896), prolific serial killer and owner of Chicago's "Murder Castle." His grave is unmarked but is in Section 15, Row 9, Plot 12, Grave 1, between Ellen Cordy and Giacomo Pipito, at GPS 39.92734, -75.25756, although some relatives believe he's not there. See "The Devil in the City of Brotherly Love" (Center City Philadelphia).

- **Angelo Bruno** (1910–1980), long-time boss of the Philadelphia mob. Section 23, Row 2, Plot 16, or GPS 39.93237, -75.25663. See "Not-So-Gentle Death of a Don" (South Philadelphia).

- **Philip "Chicken Man" Testa** (1924–1981), Philly mob boss. Section 21, Row 3, Plot 29, or GPS 39.93145, -75.25564. See "Chicken Take-Out" (South Philadelphia).

- **The Deering Family,** victims of a senseless slaughter by a worker on their farm in 1866. Their mass grave is below the large marble marker with a statue of the Virgin Mary in Section 14, or GPS 39.92632, -75.25763. Inscriptions on the side panels refer to re-burial from St. Mary's Cemetery. See "The First Ward Horror" (South Philadelphia).

3

THE MOLLY MAGUIRES

Molly Maguire might have been an elderly Irish woman evicted by her British landlord, or maybe the owner of a tavern where vigilantes met before attacking their English foes. Fact is, nobody truly knows where the name of this infamous and secret Irish society originated.

Although generations have spoken the name in the northeastern Pennsylvania coal fields, the Molly Maguires are an elusive lot. As with much of the turbulent struggle between the Irish coalminers and their Welsh/English bosses in the late 1800s, the truth is as murky as an Irish bog. But it's safe to say that atrocities and murders were committed by both sides, and the fine line between good guys and bad guys is as mysterious as the Mollies.

At the time many of America's mine workers were Irish immigrants, escaping the potato famine that killed a million people in Ireland in the mid-1800s. But life in this new land wasn't much easier. They looked for work but found signs with "No Irish Need Apply" in the windows of many businesses. Among the few jobs the Irish could take were those in coal mines, where work was dangerous and dreary. But they soon discovered that, just like back home, the hated English and Welsh were in control, this time as mine owners and bosses.

The anthracite coal regions of Schuylkill, Carbon, Columbia, and Northumberland counties were little more than fiefdoms. The mining companies owned the small communities, or "patches," where the miners lived and forced them to buy their supplies from the company store, where prices were inflated

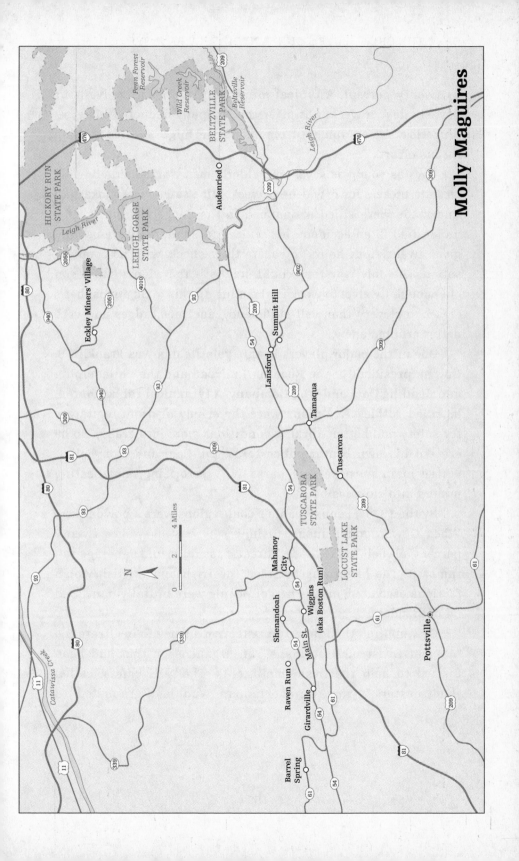

Molly Maguires

by twenty percent. A typical miner would work a twelve-hour day, six days a week. But after the company deducted his rent, groceries, and equipment from his pay, he might receive nothing for his efforts.

Boys as young as seven and elderly men worked side-by-side as slate-pickers for fifty cents a week. Mine safety was a joke, and thousands were killed or maimed in the dangerous mines. If a miner died in an accident, his widow and children were usually given twenty-four hours to vacate their shack, with no compensation. The only way they could stay is if the widow had a son old enough (twelve) to work in the mine. In this toxic atmosphere, closer to slavery than self-sufficiency, ancient grudges and vendettas erupted anew.

One of the major players in this volatile mix was Franklin B. Gowen, president of the Reading Railroad and the Philadelphia and Reading Coal and Iron Company. A tyrannical robber-baron, he ruled ruthlessly. Unions were the enemy of profit; agitators for safety and better working conditions were intolerable. So he created his own brutal police force, the Coal and Iron Police, whose main purpose was harassing, terrorizing, and beating miners into submission.

By the 1870s, Pennsylvania's coal regions were a powder keg. When Gowen added insult to injury by cutting wages twenty percent, all hell broke loose. Threats, assaults, and sabotage ran rampant. The bitterness between the Irish and English/Welsh factions escalated, and scores of people were brutally murdered on both sides.

Gowen hired the Pinkerton Detective Agency to infiltrate the "Ancient Order of Hibernians," an organization that had been formed to help the Irish immigrants. The AOH chiefs, called "bodymasters," were former miners who had graduated to owning taverns or other businesses and had become prominent men in the mining towns. Gowen claimed the AOH was a front for the "Molly Maguires" and that it was responsible for the raging violence.

Allen Pinkerton appointed his best detective, James McParland, to go undercover. Using the alias "James McKenna," McParland worked for more than two years on the case, drifting from town to town, pretending to be an out-of-work miner, counterfeiter, and fugitive killer while he collected evidence on the Mollies. He soon worked his way into the AOH inner circle and sent daily reports of their activities to his agency superiors. When it was over twenty men went to the gallows, dozens more went to prison, and the Mollies were effectively snuffed.

THE BEATING OF FRANK W. S. LANGDON
Audenreid
Hamburger's Stables stood on the site of the boarded-up former Methodist Episcopal Church on the east side of Route 309, or GPS 40.91377, -75.99243.

On June 14, 1862, mine foreman Frank W. S. Langdon delivered a derogatory speech against Irish miners at the Williams Hotel (now a vacant lot) on the east side of Route 309, just past the county line at GPS 40.91434, -75.99264. After the speech John "Black Jack" Kehoe, who'd one day become the reputed "King of the Mollies," was overheard muttering a threat against Langdon. That night Langdon was found badly beaten in the stables. He died three days later.

At Kehoe's trial fifteen years later, witnesses claimed to have seen him and other Irishmen drinking at Bach's Tavern (still standing but now a private home) at 201 Tamaqua Street (GPS

40.91037, -75.99138), which would have required them to pass those stables. That and the supposed threat were enough "evidence" to hang Kehoe. Langdon's murder was the first attributed to the Mollies.

THE AMBUSH OF ALEXANDER REA
Barrel Spring

Route 61 South, between Mount Carmel and Centralia. Look for a sports club's faded sign on the right at GPS 40.79996, -76.37675. Stop here and go up the trail past a pond to a dry creek bed at GPS 40.79934, -76.37656.

On October 17, 1868, mine superintendent Alexander Rea was ambushed by four Irishmen who believed he carried the company payroll. They dragged him into the woods and shot him, then searched his corpse for the money. They were a day late. The payroll had been delivered the day before. They stole his wallet and watch instead. Patrick Hester, Peter McHugh, and Patrick Tully were later executed for the crime. The fourth man turned state's evidence.

BLACKLISTING REVENGE
Lansford

The former Lehigh and New England Railroad Station is on Dock Street, a sharp left off the bottom of Klocks Hill Road, or GPS 40.83319, -75.88603.

Welsh mine-superintendent John P. Jones had blacklisted an Irish miner, preventing him from getting work. For this Jones was killed here on September 3, 1875, allegedly by Alexander Campbell, Michael Doyle, and Edward Kelly, who were all hanged for the murder. Jones is buried near Benjamin Yost in Odd Fellows Cemetery,

Tamaqua. His grave is fifty feet northeast of Soldiers Circle, or GPS 40.79636, -75.98062.

A DEADLY FIRE-FIGHT
Mahanoy City
9 West Railroad Street, across from the railroad bridge, or GPS 40.81319, -76.14195.

The animosity between Welsh and Irish was so great that they maintained separate fire-fighting brigades, which would extinguish fires only in their own districts. On October 31, 1874, a blaze broke out downtown, precisely between the rival territories. Both companies arrived, but instead of fighting the fire, they fought each other. When City Burgess George Major, a Welshman, tried to restore order, Irishman John McCann shot him to death.

A DOUBLE MURDER
Raven Run
Cuyler's Colliery stood to the northwest of the former mining patch at GPS 40.81687, -76.25587. A gate at the site now leads to a modern strip-mine on private property.

On September 1, 1875, English mine foreman Thomas Sanger was walking to work with his miner friend, William Uren, when both were shot and killed, allegedly by Thomas Munley, Dennis Donnelly, Charles and James (aka "Friday") O'Donnell, and Charles and James McAllister. The first two Irishmen would later be executed for the crime; the other four got retribution of another sort (see the entry below on the Wiggins Patch Massacre). Sanger and Uren are buried in the Sanger family plot at Odd Fellows Cemetery, Wildcat Road, Girardville. Turn right off 2nd Street onto Wildcat Road and drive to the cemetery on the right. Stop and walk halfway up the open walkway from Wildcat Road (not the front gate) and search for "Sanger" written in tile on a ground enclosure to the left. Sanger's headstone is close to the walkway at GPS 40.79861, -76.27763. Uren's grave is unmarked.

A GUNMAN IS GUNNED DOWN
Shenandoah

Glover's Grove, 969 West Penn Street, just outside Shenandoah, or GPS 40.82109, -76.21410.

On August 11, 1873, as Irishman Edward Cosgrove stood on the southwest corner of Main and Centre Streets (GPS 40.82038, -76.20130), he was shot to death by Gomer James. The Welshman claimed self-defense and was acquitted, but that didn't satisfy his Irish enemies.

Two years later, on August 14, 1875, James was tending bar at a picnic in this grove when he was gunned down by Irishman Thomas Hurley. James is buried at Odd Fellows Cemetery, 36 Cemetery Road. His grave is at the first right turn past the circle on the left entrance road, at GPS 40.82776, -76.21030.

MORGAN POWELL SLAIN
Summit Hill

The murder scene is in front of 146 West Ludlow Street, or GPS 40.82406, -75.87425. This is private property.

Welshman Morgan Powell was a mine boss who preferred giving jobs to Welshmen, not the Irish. His hiring preference got him killed on December 2, 1871. The alleged killers, John "Yellow Jack" Donahue, Alexander Campbell, and Thomas Fisher, were all hanged later for the slaying. Powell (1827–1871) is buried under a large monument at Summit Hill Memorial Park, North Chestnut and Union streets (GPS 40.82713, -75.87198). His monument is near the back wall of the cemetery, at GPS 40.82672, -75.87342.

A COP KILLING
Tamaqua

Northwest corner of West Broad and North Lehigh Streets, or GPS 40.79664, -75.97768. A historical marker and an old-fashioned streetlamp mark the site.

Benjamin Yost, a Civil War veteran and patrolman who had previously tangled with the Mollies, was fatally shot on July 6, 1875, as he extinguished a gas streetlamp. He was carried to his home nearby at 8 South Lehigh Street (GPS 40.79615, -75.97753), where he died the next day. James Boyle, James Carroll, Thomas Duffy, and James Roarity were later hanged for his murder. Yost is buried at Odd Fellows Cemetery, 503 West Broad Street. The grave is twenty-five feet west of Soldiers Circle, near a large concrete cross, at GPS 40.79615, -75.98148. His portrait is on his tombstone.

WIGGINS PATCH MASSACRE
Wiggins (aka Boston Run)

1247 West Centre Street, or GPS 40.80330, -76.18833. The sagging old house recently became a road hazard and was torn down, but some ruins remain. This is private property.

Elderly widow Margaret O'Donnell operated a boarding house where her pregnant daughter, Ellen, lived with her husband, Charles McAllister. Also staying there were Margaret's two sons, Charles and Friday O'Donnell, James McAllister, and four unrelated male boarders. The two sets of brothers were suspected "Mollies" identified by Pinkerton detective James McParland in one of his reports, which was leaked by his superiors to the Welsh faction.

On December 10, 1875, masked intruders stormed the house in the middle of the night, grabbed Charles and Friday O'Donnell and James McAllister, and dragged them outside. Even with a rope around his neck, McAllister broke free and ran, shot in his arm as he fled. Friday also got away, but his brother wasn't so lucky. The intruders shot Charles O'Donnell fifteen times in such rapid succession that his clothing caught fire as he died.

The noise awoke Ellen, who was shot to death as she came downstairs to investigate, her unborn child dying with her. Before the raiders left they brutally pistol-whipped the aged Margaret.

McParland was enraged by the brutality against the women and threatened to quit. No one was ever brought to justice for the massacre.

The O'Donnells and Ellen McAllister are buried together at Old St. Jerome's Cemetery, adjacent to Mahanoy, Nescopec, and High Streets in Tamaqua. Their white square stone can be seen just inside the fence, halfway up the High Street side of the cemetery at GPS 40.79554, -75.97338.

Also at Old St. Jerome's is **John "Black Jack" Kehoe** (1837–1878) who was related by marriage to the O'Donnells. He's on the

Platform overlooking the grave of John "Black Jack" Kehoe, King of the Mollies

opposite side of the graveyard, near the back. Since the cemetery is always locked, a viewing platform at GPS 40.79590, -75.97364 was built on the Mahanoy Street side to enable visitors to see Kehoe's gravestone from behind the fence.

THE END OF THE MOLLIES

By early 1876, detective James McParland believed he was targeted for death and left Pennsylvania's coal fields. Railroad president Franklin Gowen, formerly a district attorney, ordered the arrest of scores of reputed "Mollies" and appointed himself chief prosecutor, promptly banning Irish Catholics from their juries, even as other immigrants who could barely speak English were seated. With testimony by McParland and some Irish turncoats (one actually known as "Kelly the Bum"), Gowen won the death penalty for twenty Mollies, and dozens more went to Eastern State Penitentiary in Philadelphia.

On June 21, 1877—known as "The Day of the Rope"—ten Mollies were hanged at two separate jails. At the Carbon County Jail (now the Old Jail and Museum), 128 West Broadway, Mauch Chunk (today's Jim Thorpe), GPS 40.86360, -75.74651, Alexander Campbell, Edward Kelly, Michael Doyle, and John Donahue were all hanged together. Before leaving his cell, Campbell supposedly wiped his hand on the dirty floor and placed it against his cell wall, declaring that the print would remain there forever to signify he was an innocent man. Over the years several attempts have been made to wash the handprint off, paint or plaster over it, and chip it out, but it still remains clearly visible in cell No. 17.

Thomas Fisher was hanged at the jail on March 28, 1878, and Charles Sharpe and James McDonnell followed together on January 14, 1879. Sharpe's and McDonnell's executions were stayed, but the sheriff refused to allow the messenger to enter until thirty seconds after the hangings.

*Replica of the gallows at the Carbon County Jail,
where seven Molly Maguires met their doom*

A historical marker outside tells the story of the "Mollies." It's
open for tours.

Also on June 21, 1877, at Schuylkill County Prison, 30 Sand-
erson Street in Pottsville (still functioning today at GPS 40.68800,
-76.19924), James Boyle, Thomas Duffy, Hugh McGeehan, James
Carroll, Thomas Munley, and James Roarity were all hanged simultaneously. It also has a historical marker in front. Three other

Molly Maguire historical marker outside the Carbon County Jail
JOHNSON BLUE

Mollies soon followed the first six to the gallows here, including John Kehoe on December 18, 1878. Kehoe was granted a posthumous pardon by Governor Milton Shapp a hundred years later.

Pieces of the hangman's ropes are displayed with other "Molly Maguire" memorabilia at the Schuylkill County Historical Society, 305 North Centre Street in Pottsville (GPS 40.68707, -76.19678).

Three other Mollies—Patrick Hester, Peter McHugh, and Patrick Tully—were executed together on March 25, 1878, at the now-razed Columbia County Prison in Bloomsburg. But the courthouse where the trials were held remains at 35 West Main Street, or GPS 41.00308, -76.45711.

The last Molly Maguire to hang, Peter McManus, died October 9, 1879, at the Northumberland County Jail, 39 North 2nd Street in

Northumberland County Jail, site of the hanging of the last Molly Maguire

Sunbury (GPS 40.86337, -76.79432). The courthouse where he was tried also remains at 201 Market Street in Sunbury (GPS 40.86203, -76.79461).

Most of the executed Mollies' graves are unmarked, but a few, like Kehoe's, have headstones. Two of them are:

Patrick Hester is in St. Mary's Cemetery on Locust Gap Highway in Beaverdale. The grave is at GPS 40.79112, -76.42701. James Carroll is buried in Immaculate Conception Parish Cemetery, Main Street and Sand Spring Road in Jim Thorpe. His grave is in Section C, or GPS 40.87644, -75.74173.

OTHER MOLLY MAGUIRE-RELATED SITES:

- **Hibernian House Tavern:** 21 Beech Street in Girardville, or GPS 40.79410, -76.28467. Once owned by John Kehoe and still operated by his great-grandson.

- **Columbia House Tavern:** 314 West Ridge Street in Lansford, or GPS 40.82998, -75.89123. Once owned by Alexander Campbell, it's now a private home. The murder plot against John P. Jones was reportedly hatched here.

- **Union House Tavern:** 132 East Broad Street in Tamaqua, or GPS 40.79730, -75.96831. First owned by Alexander Campbell, then by James Carroll. Benjamin Yost's murder was allegedly plotted here.

The Union House Tavern, James Carroll's saloon, where a Molly Maguire murder plot was hatched

Home of Molly Maguire prosecutor
Gen. Charles Albright

- **Charles Albright's House:** 66 Broadway in Jim Thorpe, or GPS 40.86371, -75.74023. A former Civil War general and congressman, Albright lived in this home (now housing a fancy restaurant) when, as a corporate lawyer for the local coal-mining interests, he successfully prosecuted the Molly Maguires. Appearing in court every day in his full-dress Civil War uniform (complete with gleaming sword and scabbard), he swayed the awestruck jury his way. In 1880, Albright choked on some food and went into a coma, dying soon after at age forty-nine. He's buried in Mauch Chunk Cemetery, Walnut and South Avenues in Jim Thorpe. His grave is under a brown obelisk at GPS 40.86627, -75.74127.

As Schuylkill County District Attorney,
Franklin Gowen lived in this house.

- **Franklin Gowen House:** 605 Mahantongo Street in Pottsville, or GPS 40.68235, -76.19887. Gowen lived here while he
  was Schuylkill County's district attorney and the Reading
  Railroad's lawyer. When he became president of the company, he relocated to a posh mansion in Philadelphia, which
  no longer exists.

- **Franklin Gowen's grave,** Ivy Hill Cemetery, 1201 Easton
  Road in Philadelphia, at GPS 40.07407, -75.18168. After
  destroying the Molly Maguires, Gowen soon led the Reading Railroad into bankruptcy and was deposed as president. Despondent, he committed suicide on December 13,

1889—although some passionate conspiracy theorists have speculated he was murdered.

- **John "Yellow Jack" Donahue's house:** 714 Broad Street in Tuscarora, or GPS 40.77050, -76.03648. Known as "the Body-master of Tuscarora," Donahue was hanged for the murder of Morgan Powell and likely killed Frank Langdon, too.

- **Pinkerton legend James McParland's grave,** Mount Olivet Cemetery in Wheat Ridge, Colorado, at GPS 39.78369, -105.14489. McParland's celebrity was even bigger than reality. He was so famous that Sir Arthur Conan Doyle contrived a meeting between McParland and the fictional sleuth Sherlock Holmes in his 1915 novel *The Valley of Fear.* McParland died May 18, 1919, in Denver's Mercy Hospital after a simple surgery. Newspaper eulogies pointed out that the Great Detective (as he was known by Sherlock Holmes)

Molly Maguire Memorial Park

had been the target of bombers, gunmen, arsonists, and a variety of other assassins, but persisted.

- **Molly Maguire Memorial,** southeast corner of Center and Catawissa streets in Mahanoy City, or GPS 40.81204, -76.14454. Molly Maguire Historic Park consists of a walled enclosure with black granite panels that tell the story of the conflict. The centerpiece is a large green statue of a hooded man about to be hanged, with the outline of a gallows behind him. The site at this intersection is significant since there was an unwritten law in the town that no Irishman was allowed to go any farther east on Center Street than Catawissa. If he did and was caught, he would be beaten to a bloody pulp.

- **Eckley Miners' Village,** 2 Main Street in Eckley, or GPS 40.99564, -75.85565. The 1970 film, *The Molly Maguires*, starring Sean Connery and Richard Harris—and based on a 1969 novel by Arthur H. Lewis—was filmed at this restored mining "patch," now a tourist attraction. The visitor center has a film and exhibits.

Eckley Miners' Village, where the movie The Molly Maguires *was filmed*

4

PITTSBURGH & WESTERN PENNSYLVANIA

A CHILD-KILLER'S CHILDHOOD HOME
Altoona

The trailer space is at 208 East Temple Lane, or GPS 40.54113, -78.35964. This is private property.

Everyone starts somewhere. Before she became a resident of Texas's Death Row, Darlie Lynn Peck was born and grew up in Altoona. In her teens she and her mother moved to the Lone Star State. Mama Darlie arranged a date for her daughter with a young man she worked with named Darin Routier, and the two were immediately smitten. They were soon wed and became the parents of three sons—Devon, Damon, and Drake. But the young couple lived way beyond their means, and began drowning in debt. Darlie feared losing the lifestyle she craved—large, flashy, and trashy.

On the night of June 6, 1996, six-year-old Devon and five-year-old Damon were stabbed to death in their suburban Rowlett, Texas, home, while seven-month-old baby Drake slept upstairs. Darlie, also wounded but not seriously, told police an intruder had attacked her and her two older sons with a butcher knife. But the deeper investigators delved into her story, the more they suspected Darlie herself. The murder weapon came from her kitchen, as did the knife used to cut the outside window screen. Her fancy jewelry lay untouched on the kitchen counter, and the blood evidence didn't jibe with her story.

After delivering baby Drake, Darlie suffered from postpartum depression, and had supposedly contemplated suicide a month

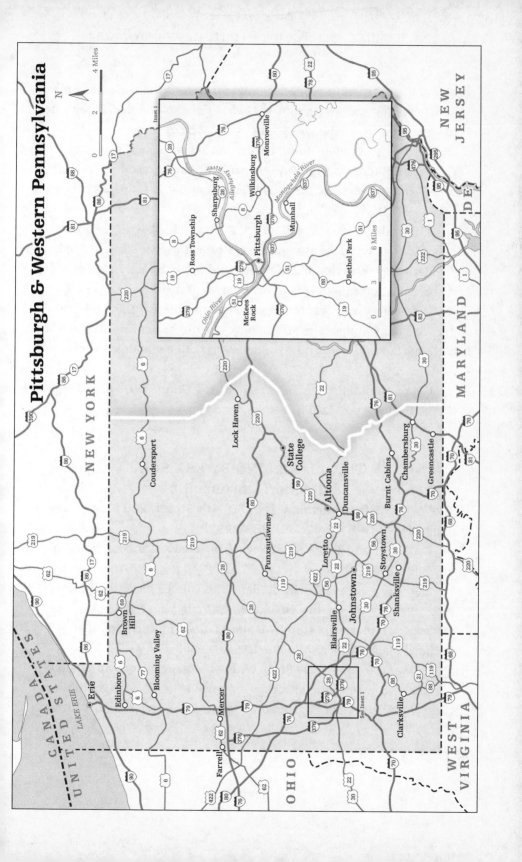

Pittsburgh & Western Pennsylvania

Inset 1

Ross Township
Sharpsburg
Allegheny River
Wilkinsburg
Monroeville
Pittsburgh
Monongahela River
Munhall
McKees Rock
Bethel Park
Ohio River

6 Miles

See Inset 1

NEW YORK

Coudersport
Lock Haven
State College
Altoona
Duncansville
Loretto
Johnstown
Blairsville
Stoystown
Shanksville
Burnt Cabins
Chambersburg
Greencastle
Punxsutawney
Brown Hill
Blooming Valley
Edinboro
Erie
Mercer
Farrell
Clarksville

LAKE ERIE

CANADA
UNITED STATES

OHIO

WEST VIRGINIA

MARYLAND

NEW JERSEY

DELAWARE

4 Miles

N

before the murder. In a note she had written at the time, she ominously apologized to her sons for "what I'm about to do." It begged the question: Just who was going to die—she or they?

Devon and Damon Routier were buried in Rest Haven Memorial Park, 2500 Texas Highway 66 East/Williams Street, in Rockwall, Texas. Their graves are in the Faith section, Lot 751, Spaces A/B, at GPS 32.93791, -96.42370.

A few days after the boys' deaths, Darlie hosted a bizarre graveside party on what would have been Devon's seventh birthday, laughing, chewing bubble gum, and spraying silly string—an odd celebration caught by a police camera. Darlie was arrested four days later and was eventually sentenced to die for Damon's murder. But many supporters still believe she did not murder the boys, and they continue to agitate for a new trial. She remains on Texas's death row.

For more details, see *The Crime Buff's Guide to Outlaw Texas* (Globe Pequot Press, 2011).

THRILL-KILLING BY THE SEA
Altoona/Duncansville

The former Sifrit apartment is at 301 6th Street, 2nd Floor, Duncansville, or GPS 40.42689, -78.42292.

Benjamin and Erika Sifrit saw themselves as a cool, modern-day Bonnie and Clyde.

She was a former honor student and college basketball player who liked living on the edge. She was also a scrapbooker and owned a scrapbooking store, "Memory Laine," in a strip mall at 415 Orchard Plaza, Suite A, Altoona (GPS 40.46802, -78.40378).

He was a former Navy SEAL with a taste for tattoos and blood.

The two twenty-somethings supported their lavish, clubbing lifestyle by burglarizing popular chain restaurants and selling their booty on eBay. On Memorial Day weekend 2002, the Pennsylvania couple went on a vacation to a luxury condo in Ocean City, Maryland.

On a transit bus to an oceanfront club called Seacrets (117 49th Street in Ocean City, or GPS 38.374533, 75.071812), the Sifrits met Joshua Ford and his girlfriend, Martha "Geney" Crutchley. The four ended up later at the Sifrits' rented penthouse at the Rainbow Condominiums for hot-tubbing and drinks.

In a bizarre turn of events, Erika accused their new friends of stealing her purse, and Ben threatened them with a gun. The frightened couple locked themselves in the bathroom and pleaded their innocence. But the Sifrits battered down the door and killed Ford and Crutchley. They were stripped of their valuables and their bodies were dismembered, stuffed in plastic garbage bags, and tossed in a grocery store Dumpster. Pieces of them were later found in a Delaware landfill.

The Sifrits were arrested a week later while burglarizing a Hooters Restaurant (12207 Coastal Highway in Ocean City, or GPS 38.427796, -75.056062). The macabre murder plot unraveled when Ford's and Crutchley's driver's licenses were found in Erika's purse. Benjamin said Erika—who proudly wore Ford's ring on her necklace—did all the killing, and he merely chopped up the bodies; Erika claimed Benjamin—who'd plotted to kill his wife's entire family for the inheritance—terrorized and killed the couple, then got a tattoo to remind himself of the bloody night.

Two juries didn't buy it, believing both were guilty. Benjamin got thirty-five years in prison for second-degree murder and other crimes related to the slayings; Erika got life plus twenty years for first-degree murder.

In 2008, Benjamin filed for divorce from Erika. Grounds? Because Erika, he said, was a convicted felon. It was granted.

AMERICA'S FIRST ARMORED-CAR ROBBERY
Bethel Park

The robbery site was the corner of Old Bethel Church Road and Library Road, or GPS 40.34496, -80.02747.

On March 11, 1927, two Brinks armored cars were transporting the payroll for the Pittsburgh Terminal Coal Company. They had already visited two mines in the area and were on their way to three more.

As the cars turned onto Library Road, an explosion erupted beneath one of them. The first car was blown seventy-five feet into the air before landing on its roof in a sixty-foot crater, knocking the driver unconscious. Seconds later, another explosion missed the second car but tipped it onto its side into another big hole.

Hidden nearby a gang called "The Flatheads" ran to the cars. They held the dazed guards at gunpoint while snatching a total of $103,834.38. But one of the guards managed to see their license plate number as they sped away, and soon cops were on their trail.

Three of the bandits, including ringleader Paul Jaworski, were soon captured while sleeping in a haystack at a nearby farm.

Jaworski was a fugitive who'd escaped from prison while awaiting execution for a series of violent robberies that had left several people dead and had netted $200,000. He bragged about killing twenty-six men. His sentence for the armored-car robbery and his other crimes was again death, but he escaped once more, killing a prison guard and wounding two others. After a bloody shoot-out in Cleveland, Jaworski was captured again, this time keeping his date with the executioner on January 21, 1929. Only $38,000 of the stolen money was ever recovered. The rest remains missing to this day.

THE WHISKEY REBELLION
Bethel Park

Bower Hill stood on Kane Boulevard, Scott Township, at GPS 40.37426, -80.08611. A historical marker is on the spot.

A hundred and thirty years before Prohibition, the new federal government got a taste of what happens when it tries to come between Americans and their booze.

In 1791, Treasurer Alexander Hamilton enacted a tax on whiskey distillers to help pay costly Revolutionary War debts. But despite its worthy purpose, the tax proved to be a lot less popular than the war itself, especially in western Pennsylvania. It unfairly penalized small farmers who couldn't produce enough of their twenty-five-cents-a-gallon liquor to make any money after the nine-cents-a-gallon tax was collected. Tempers flared, and tax collectors became an endangered species.

Revenuer Robert Johnson came into Washington County on September 11, 1791, and was promptly tarred, feathered, and literally run out of town on a rail. When another government man came to arrest Johnson's attackers, he was whipped, then also tarred, feathered, and railed. Outbreaks of vandalism and intimidation continued though 1793, with barn-burnings and threats of violence, not only on the tax collectors but on anyone who cooperated with them. John Neville, federal tax inspector for western Pennsylvania, was burned in effigy, and tax collector Benjamin Wells was forced to resign at gunpoint.

On July 15, 1794, Neville and a US Marshal came under fire at the homestead of rebel leader Oliver Miller. (The home still remains on Stone Manse Drive, east off Corrigan Drive circle, at GPS 40.32025, -80.00640). Neville retreated to his home, Bower Hill, while the marshal returned to Pittsburgh. The next day, the boiling insurrection came to a violent climax, when a large group of militants surrounded Bower Hill and called for the marshal's surrender (whom they believed was with Neville).

Neville fired at the mob, killing Oliver Miller. The rebels returned fire to no avail, then left to regroup.

The next day, the rebels returned with up to 600 men under the command of former Revolutionary War Major James McFarlane. For an hour a gun battle raged at Bower Hill, until McFarlane called for a cease-fire. As the major stepped into the open, he was shot dead by someone in the house. The enraged rebels then burned the place to the ground. Neville somehow managed to escape to his other house, Woodville, still standing at 1375 Washington Pike, Bridgeville (GPS 40.37952, -80.09635).

By then President George Washington had dispatched a force of 13,000 men to crush the rebellion, but the militants had already dispersed. The tax was repealed in 1801.

John Neville is buried at Allegheny Cemetery, 4734 Butler Street, Pittsburgh, in Section 11, Lot 21, or GPS 40.47422, -79.95225.

ANDY WARHOL'S GRAVE
Bethel Park
St. John the Baptist Byzantine Catholic Cemetery is at Connor Road and Highway 88. Warhol's grave is at GPS 40.35441, -80.02986.

Avant-garde artist Andy Warhol (1928–1987) was born in Pittsburgh to Slovakian immigrants. He grew up in a row house here, attended public school, and eventually studied fine art at Carnegie Institute of Technology in Pittsburgh.

But after he moved to New York City in 1949, he blossomed into the cultural phenomenon whose pop-art paintings of soup cans and Marilyn Monroe in quadruplicate were the rage of the 1960s and '70s. He enjoyed being a strange guy who attracted a weird mix of New Age artists, actors, and other hangers-on to the New York loft he called "The Factory."

Fans leave soup cans on Andy Warhol's grave.

One of the weirdest was would-be playwright Valerie Solanas, who had loaned him her latest script, which bore the charming title of *Up Your Ass*.

On June 3, 1968, she came to the loft to retrieve it from him, but Warhol flippantly told her he'd lost it. She stormed out, stewing over her "lost" chance at Broadway stardom. Returning later with a gun, she shot Warhol three times, seriously wounding him. He almost died on the operating table but survived. Solanas (1936–1988) was sentenced to three years in prison (including one she served in a mental hospital).

Although Warhol eventually recovered, he was never physically well again, dying at age fifty-nine from complications of gall-bladder surgery.

Warhol once said that everyone would have fifteen minutes of fame. His fame has lasted much longer. His grave is visited often by his fans, who leave mementos and cans of soup at the site.

Warhol's childhood home is at 3252 Dawson Street in South Oakland (GPS 40.431274, -79.953760). It's privately owned and not a museum.

The Andy Warhol Museum in Pittsburgh is at 117 Sandusky Street, just across the Andy Warhol Bridge from downtown (GPS 40.448506, -80.002653). Hours are 10 a.m. to 5 p.m. Tuesday through Sunday. Admission is charged.

ANOTHER DEADLY DIVORCE
Blairsville
The former Yelenic home is at 233 South Spring Street, or GPS 40.42759, -79.26575. This is private property.

When prominent dentist Dr. John Yelenic was found beaten and stabbed to death inside his house on April 13, 2006, police didn't have to go far to find a suspect. The doctor and his wife, Michele, had been embroiled in a bitter, four-year-long divorce and custody battle.

Michele's live-in lover, Pennsylvania State Policeman Kevin Foley, had frequently wished aloud to his fellow troopers that Yelenic was dead, even going so far as to ask one of them to help kill him. But no one reported Foley to his superiors or warned Yelenic.

The acrimonious divorce was to be granted one day after Yelenic died, but the dentist's unsigned papers were found splattered with his blood at the crime scene.

The circumstantial evidence against Foley was overwhelming: He hated the dentist; his brand of sneakers made bloody footprints at the house; the pocket-knife he had habitually flicked open and shut every day, even at roll-call, mysteriously disappeared the day after the murder; the security tape at a gas station showed a car like his going toward Yelenic's house; a cut on his forehead was visible on the morning after the murder; and his girlfriend stood to gain two million dollars if Yelenic died before the divorce went through.

Still, it took a year and a half before Foley was arrested. Yelenic's family blamed the state police for stonewalling and filed a one million dollar lawsuit against them.

At the trial the jury was out for only six hours. Foley was convicted and got life in prison. Michele never appeared in court and moved out of town after the trial, abandoning her love nest to creditors. She relinquished all claim to her late husband's estate money and was never charged in the crime.

Dr. Yelenic (1967–2006) is buried at Blairsville Cemetery, 609 East Market Street in Blairsville.

A TROUBLED POLITICO'S GRAVE
Blooming Valley

Blooming Valley Cemetery is on Saegertown Street, between Cemetery Road and Linda Avenue. Dwyer's grave marker, shaped like a keystone, is at GPS 41.68404, -80.04605.

On January 22, 1987, disgraced Pennsylvania State Treasurer Robert "Bud" Dwyer had just been convicted of bribery. Out on bail the day before his sentencing, he called a press conference inside the Treasury at 129 Finance Building in Harrisburg (GPS 40.26603, -76.88126).

After reading a prepared statement declaring his innocence, he handed a sealed envelope to each of his three aides. Reaching for another large envelope, he pulled out a .357 Magnum pistol. Brandishing it before the horrified media, he warned anyone who might be squeamish to leave. Despite urgent pleas to put the gun away, he stuck it in his mouth and pulled the trigger, spraying his brains on the wall behind him.

When his aides opened the envelopes, they found one had a suicide note to his wife, one contained an organ-donor card, and the last one contained a letter to new governor Robert Casey. The grisly footage was shown in its entirety on only one local news station, but it soon made it onto the Internet, where it's been viewed by millions.

"THE MOUNTAIN MAN"
Burnt Cabins

The former Rubeck house is at 31210 Route 522 North, or GPS 40.06325, -77.94614. This is private property.

In the mid-1960s, a masked intruder terrorized the rural hamlets of Burnt Cabins and Shade Gap by shooting into houses, attacking locals on their porches, and firing at cars. In one case, dressed only in a mask and raincoat, he kicked down a door, grabbed the woman inside, and raped her in the nearby cornfield.

The culprit was nicknamed "The Mountain Man" because, after each assault, he would disappear into the neighboring mountains. The small local police force couldn't find him, and the assailant eluded justice for two years.

At the same time, a local eccentric the kids called "Bicycle Pete" was seen riding his bike through the countryside with a white dog in the basket. No one knew him, and he spoke to no one. He seemed harmless, and everyone left him alone. What they didn't know was that he was a former mental patient and ex-con named William Hollenbaugh . . . and that he was the mysterious "Mountain Man." But his anonymity was soon to change.

On May 11, 1966, seventeen-year-old Peggy Ann Bradnick got off the school bus with her younger brothers and sisters, and they began the half-mile walk to their home. Without warning a man wearing goggles and holding a rifle stepped out of the roadside trees and grabbed Peggy, whisking her away before her siblings' startled eyes. The children ran home to tell their father, who got his gun and went looking for her. A desperate call to police sparked the largest manhunt in Pennsylvania history, with the FBI, state troopers, local cops, armed citizens, and everybody from state game

The memorial to slain FBI agent, Terry Anderson

wardens to National Guardsmen volunteering their services—a thousand people in all.

A command center was established at Shade Gap picnic grounds (now Harpers Memorial Park) on Route 641 in Shade Gap (GPS 40.18203, -77.85807) and a strategy was mapped out inside a large metal building there (GPS 40.17889, -77.86079). For five days the assembled lawmen forayed into the mountains but found no sign of Peggy or her abductor.

On the sixth day an expert tracker from Arkansas and his prized German Shepherds, Weid and King, joined the search. The dogs caught a scent and led the tracker, FBI Agent Terry Anderson, and a state trooper to the summit of a steep hill called Gobbler's Knob.

There they spotted Bicycle Pete's white dog in a clearing. As they approached it a shotgun-wielding Hollenbaugh appeared.

Agent Anderson and Weid were shot and killed. King was shot but survived, and Hollenbaugh escaped with Peggy.

Hollenbaugh dragged Peggy to the outhouse of a rustic cabin off the left side of Route 522 North, through a cattle gate at GPS 40.06332, -77.94643 and up a dirt road, just south of the Rubeck house. They spent the night there, unaware that Deputy Sheriff Francis Sharpe had commandeered the nearby cabin as a place to sleep.

When Sharpe went to the outhouse the next morning, Hollenbaugh shot him in the stomach, and then ordered him to take them out of there. Sharpe, wounded but alive, drove the fugitive and his hostage down the path toward Route 522. But at the gate the deputy alerted nearby searchers and a gun battle erupted.

Hollenbaugh, with Peggy stumbling behind him, was wounded in the back as he sprinted toward a barn. He faltered, and then turned toward the Rubeck house with his gun raised. Another few shots rang out, and Hollenbaugh fell dead.

Peggy and the deputy were treated and survived. Peggy later told the police and reporters that Hollenbaugh had punched her and fondled her a few times but didn't rape her. To prevent her from escaping at night, he chained her to trees.

In 2011, forty-five years after Peggy's abduction, a memorial marker dedicated to slain FBI Agent Terry Anderson was erected at Shade Gap Presbyterian Church, Route 522, near the intersection with Route 193 in Shade Gap (GPS 40.18270, -77.86180). Peggy Ann Bradnick Jackson was at the ceremony to honor the man who gave his life to rescue her.

Anderson was buried in Washington, Iowa, where he was born.

The crime was retold in a 1991 made-for-TV movie, *Cry in the Wild: The Taking of Peggy Ann*, starring Megan Follows, David Morse, and David Soul, and in the book *Deadly Pursuit* by Robert Cox.

JOHN BROWN'S LAST HOME
Chambersburg

The John Brown House is at 225 East King Street, or GPS 39.93879, -77.65826. It offers tours from 10 a.m. to 4 p.m. Tuesday through Saturday. Admission is charged.

Using the alias Dr. Isaac Smith, radical abolitionist John Brown rented rooms in this boarding house just before his disastrous raid on Harper's Ferry. He had already helped create "Bloody Kansas" over the issue of slavery, and he now sent word to his wealthy supporters that he needed weapons so he could lead a force of 4,500 men to attack the federal armory in Virginia (now West Virginia). His plan was to start an armed slave insurrection in the southern states.

Inside this house, abolitionist John Brown made plans to invade Harper's Ferry.

As a result of his pleas, he soon received two hundred rifles, a supply of ammunition, and, strangely, nearly one thousand six-foot-long metal pikes at this small, unassuming house that sits just fifteen miles north of the Mason-Dixon line. While here, Brown met secretly with fellow abolitionist Frederick Douglass in a nearby quarry, trying unsuccessfully to get him to join the raid.

On the day of the attack, October 16, 1859, Brown had managed to scrounge up only twenty-one men to go with him. Undaunted, he and his die-hards advanced on the armory, which was, incredibly, guarded by only one watchman.

After some initial success the invaders were soon besieged inside a small firehouse by federal troops commanded by Colonel Robert E. Lee. Gunfire was exchanged. Brown's men killed four soldiers and wounded nine more. But the federals killed ten, including Brown's sons, Watson and Oliver. Brown and six others were captured as five escaped.

The anti-slavery zealot was tried and sentenced to be hanged. Before his execution, he wrote a prophetic note: "I, John Brown, am now quite certain that the crimes of this guilty land will never be purged away, but with blood."

The Civil War, waged largely over the issue of slavery, broke out two years later and was the bloodiest conflict in American history.

Brown was buried at the John Brown Farm Grounds in North Elba, New York (GPS 44.25197, -73.97095).

THE YABLONSKI FAMILY MASSACRE
Clarksville

The Yablonskis' murder scene is west of town on Bridge Avenue, or GPS 39.97801, -80.04537. This is private property.

In 1969, W. A. "Tony" Boyle was the powerful and corrupt boss of the United Mineworkers Union. When his former colleague, Joseph

The murders of the Yablonski family took place inside their home.

"Jock" Yablonski, accused him of embezzling and ran against him for the leadership of the union, Boyle was furious.

Boyle won the election by a two-to-one margin, but Yablonski claimed fraud and asked the US Labor Department to investigate. Now even more enraged, Boyle paid $20,000 to his executive councilman Albert Pass to "take care" of Yablonski. The order trickled down the union hierarchy until it landed in the laps of three goons—Paul Gilly, Aubran "Buddy" Martin, and Claude Vealey. They might as well have hired the Three Stooges.

The would-be hitmen followed Jock around for weeks, but their untimely beer runs and broken-down cars caused them to miss him at every turn. Staking out his home on several occasions from a nearby hill, they left their fingerprints on the beer cans they tossed out the car window. Once, they even showed up at his door, pretending to be out-of-work mineworkers, but they got cold feet and ran when Yablonski was standing right in front of them.

As time passed pressure for action grew. Finally, in the wee hours of December 31, 1969, the three thugs broke into the Yablonskis' colonial farmhouse and shot Jock, his wife, Margaret, and daughter Charlotte. The bodies were found a week later.

The incompetent assassins were captured by the police within three weeks. Martin was the first to turn state's evidence, implicating the other two and some guy named "Tony." It took almost five more years to get enough evidence on Tony Boyle to bring him to justice; he received three consecutive life terms and died in prison on May 3, 1985. Gilly and Vealey got the death penalty, and Martin got life.

The Yablonskis are buried at Washington Cemetery, 498 Park Avenue in Washington, Pennsylvania. Their graves are in Section 6, along the road, or GPS 40.15503, -80.25275.

There's also a historical marker about the Yablonski murders at 3rd and Wood Streets in California, Pennsylvania (GPS 40.06657, -79.88993).

END OF THE "UNTOUCHABLE"
Coudersport

Ness's former house is at 107 East 3rd Street, or GPS 41.77551, -78.01901. This is private property.

Eliot Ness (1903–1957) was one of the most famous lawmen of his day—the Treasury agent who helped bring down mobster Al Capone with his force of dedicated, incorruptible agents known as "The Untouchables."

But Ness's success in Chicago didn't follow him to his next assignment as the public safety director in Cleveland. During his time there an unidentified killer known as the "Mad Butcher of Kingsbury Run" left twelve dead and mutilated bodies all over the city. He was never caught, and Ness left Cleveland defeated.

After a raft of less glamorous jobs, Ness was hired by an anti-counterfeiting paper company in Coudersport, where he drifted

Famous G-Man Eliot Ness

into near-obscurity, settling with his wife and adopted son in this rental home.

Writer Oscar Fraley visited Ness in Coudersport years later and interviewed him about his glory days fighting mobsters in old Chicago. They met at the Hotel Crittenden, 133 North Main Street (GPS 41.77450, -78.02113), where Ness regaled Fraley with stories over a few drinks. Ness, despite his years dutifully enforcing the Prohibition laws, was now an alcoholic and had a favorite table in the back corner where he downed his booze. He also had an office at the northwest corner of 2nd and Main Streets (GPS 41.77474, -78.02112), across the street from the hotel in what is now the Fastenal building.

Fraley turned his interviews with Ness into a best-selling book, *The Untouchables*, which was later made into a popular TV series and movie. But Ness wouldn't live to see the tremendous success

Eliot Ness's final home

the book attained, nor the fame it brought him. He died of a massive heart attack at this house on May 16, 1957, at age fifty-four. He's buried at Lake View Cemetery in Cleveland, Ohio; his grave is in Section 7, Lot 8 (GPS 41.513763, -81.592365).

"SOMETHING MEMORABLE"
Edinboro

Nick's Place is at 12250 Route 99, or GPS 41.89981, -80.12725.

When fourteen-year-old Andrew Wurst told his classmates at Parker Middle School that he was going to do "something memorable" at the upcoming eighth-grade dance, they rolled their eyes. They'd heard it all before. He was always yapping about going on a crime spree or committing suicide. No one took him seriously.

But the night of the dance, April 24, 1998, he arrived at Nick's Place banquet hall with his date—a .25-caliber pistol. His first target was science teacher John Gillette. Shot twice, Gillette died on the back porch. Andrew then barged into the hall and began firing, wounding two students and another teacher, before being subdued by the shotgun-wielding hall owner.

He pleaded guilty to the shootings and was sentenced to between thirty and sixty years in prison, where he remains today.

John Gillette (1949–1998) is buried in the Laurel Hill Cemetery, 4523 Love Road in Millcreek Township.

THE COLLAR-BOMB ROBBERY
Erie

Eyeglass World is at 7360 Peach Street, or GPS 42.05298, -80.08597.

Marjorie Diehl-Armstrong wanted her father dead. He had cheated her out of her inheritance when her mother died. So she concocted one of the most convoluted and bizarre plots in the annals of crime: She and her cohorts, Kenneth Barnes and William Rothstein, would convince their friend Brian Wells to wear what he would think was a fake bomb and rob a bank, so she could get $250,000 to hire a hit man to bump off dear old Dad.

On August 28, 2003, the trio called Wells at his job at Mama Mia's Pizzeria, 5154 Peach Street (GPS 42.07843, -80.09198), and asked him to bring two pizzas to them at 8631 Peach Street (GPS 42.03756, -80.06211), the site of WSEE-TV's transmission tower.

When he arrived at the address, they jumped him and attached a real bomb with a locked metal collar around his neck. Telling him he had only an hour before the bomb would explode, they gave him a note detailing instruction he must follow before the device was disabled. First on the list was the robbery of the PNC Bank (now a phone store at GPS 42.053707, -80.087137) at Summit Towne Center, where he was to demand $250,000 from the tellers. After that he was to go to the nearby McDonald's (GPS 42.053366, -80.086249) and look under a rock in the drive-thru for his next clue.

When Wells got to the bank, he warned the teller about the explosive and demanded the enormous sum. The teller gave him only $8,702 and he left for McDonald's. There he found instructions to go next door to Eyeglass World and tie a piece of orange tape around a fire hydrant.

As he drove to Eyeglass World, state troopers, alerted by the bank, stopped him. He told them about the bomb and pleaded with them to let him go, saying his time was running out. But they refused and forced him to sit down on the asphalt.

Wells implored them to remove the collar, declaring that he was coerced into the robbery. Three minutes before the bomb-squad arrived, the collar-bomb detonated, killing Brian instantly. Across the street at the Eat 'n' Park diner, Marjorie and Barnes watched their plan literally go up in smoke and then high-tailed it out of the area. Rothstein, who was waiting at the eyeglass store to get money from Wells, snuck away unseen.

The strange incident remained a mystery for almost two years. Meanwhile, a month after the crime, police got a bizarre call from Rothstein. He told them that he had been keeping a body for Marjorie in his freezer, and he wanted the cops to remove it.

When police arrived at the tipster's house at 8645 Peach Street (GPS 42.03554, -80.06541), they noticed it was next to the television tower where Wells had taken the pizza. The body turned out to be another of Marjorie's boyfriends, James Roden, whom she had shot to death because she feared he would snitch to the cops. Marjorie was arrested and in jail she boasted to other inmates about her role in the collar-bombing.

Diehl-Armstrong and Barnes were convicted of bank robbery and Wells's murder, and sentenced to long stretches in prison. Rothstein died before he could be arrested. Ironically the riches

Diehl-Armstrong had intended to get from her father had long been spent.

Wells (1956–2003) was buried in Wintergreen Gorge Cemetery, 2601 Norcross Road. His grave is in Section 1-F, on the right side, just across the road from a traffic oval, or GPS 42.10839, -79.99124. His family believes he was an innocent dupe from the start.

DILLINGER DOES HIS THING
Farrell

The former Sol J. Gully State Bank is now a closed and gutted real estate office at 823 West Broadway Avenue, or GPS 41.21422, -80.50689.

Infamous bank robber John Dillinger (1903–1934) is known for his Midwest exploits and his messy death in Chicago. But on September 12, 1933, he and six cohorts robbed this bank, scoring a take of

The former Sol J. Gully State Bank, a Dillinger target

about $15,000. He came out with a hostage, Karl Wild, who was bundled into the getaway car and later released unharmed in Ohio. Up until a few years ago, the old vault was still in the derelict building.

AMERICA'S FIRST SCHOOL SHOOTING
Greencastle

Enoch Brown State Park is at 2730 Enoch Brown Road. The school site is marked by a large monument at GPS 39.82464, -77.75375.

Shortly after the French and Indian War, tensions remained high between the Indians and white settlers in Pennsylvania, and atrocities were committed on both sides. One of the worst happened on July 26, 1764, at a log-cabin schoolhouse where schoolmaster Enoch Brown was teaching eleven pupils.

In the middle of the lesson, three Lenni Lenape braves burst through the door. Before they shot him to death and scalped him, Brown pleaded with them to spare the children. But the warriors ignored his pleas. They tomahawked and scalped all eleven of the children. Only one child—the youngest, ten-year-old Archie McCullough—survived the slaughter. Scalped and injured but still clinging to life, Archie crawled to a nearby spring and collapsed. He was found there by the local settlers and rescued from death.

When the natives returned to their tribe with their scalp bounties, the elders admonished them for cowardice for killing children. None was ever brought to justice.

Schoolmaster Brown and his students are buried in a common grave under a large granite marker at GPS 39.82433, -77.75446. The spring where Archie was found is marked by a plaque at GPS 39.82394, -77.75482.

McCullough, physically and emotionally scarred by the massacre, became a blacksmith and died in 1814 at age sixty in Lexington, Kentucky.

The site of the one-room schoolhouse where America's first school shooting occurred

INTERRACIAL KILLING SPREE
Johnstown

The Washington Street Bridge is at Washington Street and Roosevelt Boulevard, or GPS 40.33067, -78.92577.

Joseph Paul Franklin (b. 1950) was a vitriolic white supremacist. For him even the Ku Klux Klan was too tame. He hated blacks and Jews, of course, but was particularly enraged by interracial couples. Simply seeing one such couple in a *Hustler* magazine prompted him to shoot publisher Larry Flynt in 1978, paralyzing him for life.

Starting in Rockville, Maryland, where Franklin set off a bomb at the home of a Jewish family, he worked his way around the country, planting bombs and shooting at people who offended him. After attacking at least twenty-six people (including civil-rights lawyer Vernon Jordan in 1980) and killing thirteen of them, Franklin found himself in Johnstown on June 15, 1980.

Positioning himself on a hillside near the historic seven-arch bridge, he waited for a mixed-race couple (referred by him as an "MRC") to walk by.

Arthur Smothers, a twenty-two-year-old black man, and his sixteen-year-old white girlfriend, Kathleen Mikula, were about to cross the Washington Street Bridge heading into downtown when the infuriated Franklin fired at them, killing them both. Another four people would die elsewhere before Franklin was caught later in 1980.

For years, as he stood trial around the country, he revealed more and more of his crimes to the authorities. He confessed to the Johnstown killings but has never been extradited to Pennsylvania, and the final toll of his victims will probably never be known. Franklin is now on Missouri's death row.

LEO HELD GOES POSTAL
Lock Haven

The Hammermill Paper Company plant was at 904 Woods Avenue, or GPS 41.12590, -77.45955. A new factory stands there today. This is private property.

The morning of October 23, 1967, started normally enough. Leo Held and his wife, Alda, had done some laundry in their home at 52 East Anthony Street in Loganton (GPS 41.03586,

Leo Held lost a gun-battle with police outside his home.

-77.30533), then each went to their respective jobs. That day Leo carried two extra items to the office: a .45 automatic and a .38 revolver. His commute to the paper mill was seventeen minutes long, plenty of time to plan.

As he had done for nearly twenty years, he pulled his car into a space at the parking lot across from the mill, got out, and walked across the bridge to the plant. Inside Held positioned himself between the two entry doors and waited. When his boss, Carmen Edwards, came in, he pulled one of the guns and shot him in the back, killing him. Not a word had passed between them.

Leo then went upstairs to his workspace, the quality-control lab, and methodically shot at his co-workers wherever he found them. Four more were killed and four wounded before Held walked out of the plant and got back in his car.

Driving to the town's small William T. Piper Airport, 353 Proctor Street (GPS 41.13758, -77.41961) he parked his car at the office. Strolling inside—again without a word—Held approached secretary Geraldine Ramm, who had previously been part of his carpool. As she looked up at him, he began shooting. She dove for cover as six shots rang out, wounding her in several places. (Her work-bin, with a bullet-crease, is still in use today.) Thinking the incident was a sick joke, the airport manager grabbed Held by the arm and escorted him outside.

Held drove home to Loganton, but before entering his own house, he broke through the door of his across-the-street neighbors, Floyd and Donna Quiggle, at 57 East Anthony Street (GPS 41.03597, -77.30523), and shot them both as they relaxed in bed. Floyd was killed, and Donna was paralyzed. Held then helped himself to some of their guns and carried them to his house.

By now police were on Held's trail. When two officers pulled up outside the Held house, a new gun battle ensued. Held was wounded and died in the hospital two days later. On his deathbed he said all of his victims had irked him somehow, and he regretted that he hadn't been able to shoot one more, a seventy-year-old neighbor.

Held and his last victim, Floyd Quiggle, are both buried at Fairview Cemetery, East Main Street, Loganton. Held's grave is at GPS 41.03643, -77.29831; Quiggle's is at GPS 41.03613, -77.29825.

HARRY THAW OVERHEATS
Loretto

The former Thaw "summer cottage" Elmhurst is at 365 McConnell Road, or GPS 40.46833, -78.61613. This is private property.

Harry Thaw was a little unhinged. Luckily for him, his family's coal and railroad millions usually kept him out of trouble . . . until June 25, 1906.

Evelyn Nesbit and Harry Thaw

It started when Thaw learned that before they were married, his beautiful chorus-girl wife, Evelyn Nesbit, had been deflowered by famous architect Stanford White. Thaw shot White to death during a dinner show at New York's Madison Square Garden, a landmark that White had designed. Thaw was judged insane at his trial—one of the first to be called the "trial of the century"—and sent to a mental institution, where he stayed for only five years.

But, in happier times, he and Evelyn enjoyed the pleasures of their magnificent Tudor-style summer home, which still stands and can be seen from outside the front gate. It's now a private home.

Thaw is buried at Allegheny Cemetery, 4734 Butler Street, Pittsburgh. The grave is in Section 16, Lot 119, or GPS 40.47118, -79.95077.

Harry Thaw and Evelyn Nesbit lived in this magnificent summer home.

THE MAD BUTCHER STRIKES AGAIN?
McKees Rocks

The Pittsburgh and Lake Erie Railroad Yards are at the dead-end of Linden Avenue, just north of Locust Street, or GPS 40.46763, -80.05864.

The "Mad Butcher of Kingsbury Run" had a field day in Cleveland, leaving twelve headless, mutilated bodies in his wake and destroying the career of Eliot Ness before mysteriously ending his own serial-killing career in 1938.

But, on May 3, 1940, three similar murders were discovered at the railroad yards. The headless bodies of two men and a woman were found inside boxcars of a train that had recently arrived from Ohio. One of the males had the word "NAZI" carved into his chest. Despite an intensive investigation there was no resolution to the crimes, and, like all the Cleveland killings even super-cop Ness couldn't crack, they remain unsolved.

See also "The End of the 'Untouchable'" (Coudersport).

PROSECUTING THE LINCOLN CONSPIRATORS
Mercer

The former Bingham house is at 124 South Diamond Street, or GPS 41.22649, -80.23878. It's now the local Republican headquarters.

In 1865, Mercer-born John Armour Bingham was a special military prosecutor who questioned witnesses at the trial of the three men and one woman who were involved in the conspiracy with John Wilkes Booth to kill the heads of the US government. The four—David Herold, George Atzerodt, Lewis Payne (aka Powell), and Mary Surratt—were convicted shortly after Bingham made the prosecutorial summation. All were executed.

Bingham was also a participant in the impeachment trial of President Andrew Johnson, and played an instrumental role in passing the Fourteenth Amendment, which guarantees equal protection to all people, regardless of race.

Bingham (1815–1900) is buried in Cadiz, Ohio.

BRAVERY IS NON-PARTISAN
Mercer

Congressman George Burd (1788–1844) is buried at Old Mercer Graveyard, North Erie and North Streets. The grave is at GPS 41.22970, -80.24071.

Elected to Congress as an Anti-Jacksonian candidate, Representative George Burd didn't exactly see eye-to-eye with President Andrew Jackson. In fact, they were entrenched political enemies.

On January 30, 1835, the two men were part of a large delegation of dignitaries at the funeral of Congressman Warren Davis inside the US Capitol rotunda. After the services were over, the illustrious cortege emerged onto the east portico, where a lunatic named Richard Lawrence was waiting behind a column, clutching a loaded pistol in each hand. Thinking in his deluded mind that he was the King of England, Lawrence was determined to reclaim his American colonies.

As he stepped out into the open, he took aim at the president with one of the guns and pulled the trigger. Nothing happened. Dropping that gun, he switched to the other one and tried to fire point-blank at the now-enraged Jackson's chest. But that pistol also misfired.

As the feisty president began beating the would-be assassin with his cane, other members of the entourage moved to subdue the assailant or pull Jackson off of him. Despite their political animosity, Burd helped save Jackson's life by lunging at the guns and keeping them out of Lawrence's grasp. Ironically Lawrence had test-fired the pistols the day before, and both had worked perfectly.

At the time shooting at a president was only a misdemeanor. So to ensure Lawrence would be locked up for life, he was declared insane and placed in the Government Hospital for the Insane in Washington, DC. Later, Garfield assassin Charles Guiteau and would-be Reagan assassin John Hinckley would both live in the historic hospital, now known as St. Elizabeth's.

KENT STATE VICTIM'S GRAVE
Monroeville
Betty Rosenberg Parkway Jewish Center Cemetery is just northeast of Negley Avenue and Curry Street. Allison's grave is halfway down the lone aisle on the left at GPS 40.42232, -79.82547.

Like many campuses during the Vietnam War, Kent State University in Ohio was a powder-keg. For days, hundreds of anti-war demonstrators had taken over, setting fire to the ROTC building and looting nearby businesses. The mayor called the National Guard to restore order, but their presence only fueled the fire, leading to a deadly confrontation.

On May 4, 1970, two thousand demonstrators met an armed National Guard force on the campus. Guardsmen fired tear gas, but the wind dispersed its effect. Protesters lobbed the gas canisters back at the soldiers and others threw rocks. So the Guardsmen advanced toward the rioters with bayonets fixed.

Then suddenly a shot was fired. Soldiers began firing into the crowd, killing four students and wounding nine others. One of the dead was Allison Krause, a nineteen-year-old honor student from Maryland. Her mother lived in Monroeville, so she was buried here. Just days before her death, Allison had said, "Flowers are better than bullets." It became her epitaph, etched into her headstone.

KING OF THE ROBBER BARONS
Munhall

The site of the former Homestead Steel Works is at 880 East Waterfront Drive, or GPS 40.41276, -79.89703. The only building remaining from the strike is the old pump house at GPS 40.41308, -79.89677.

Known in his day as "The Most Hated Man in America," steel magnate Henry Clay Frick made his fortune turning coal into "coke," a key ingredient in the steel industry. This endeavor led him into a prickly partnership with Andrew Carnegie, whose Carnegie Steel Company was the leading steel-maker in America. Frick became chairman of the company and ruled it with an iron fist.

His first claim to infamy began in 1881, when he led a group of wealthy industrialists who bought a dilapidated earthen dam and had it shoddily patched together to create a millionaires' club and lake resort. In spite of dire warnings from engineers that the dam was a lethal hazard, Frick refused to spend the money to shore it up properly. On May 31, 1889, the dam burst, causing the Great Johnstown Flood that killed 2,209 people and caused $17 million in property damage.

Victims' families sued the club for criminal negligence, but Frick's lawyers successfully fended them off. Not a penny was paid in restitution, although Frick contributed a paltry $5,000 to the Johnstown Relief Fund. His personal fortune at the time was $100 million.

Destruction after the historic 1889 Johnstown Flood, which killed 2,209 people

A poignant reminder of the negligence lies in the Grand-view Cemetery, 801 Millcreek Road in Johnstown. In a solemn area known as the "Unknown Plot" (GPS 40.315553, -78.927475) 777 victims lie unclaimed and unrecognized from the disaster. In all, 1,222 flood victims—more than half the dead—are buried in Grandview.

The next episode in Frick's checkered life happened three years later, when negotiations with the steelworkers' union broke down. At the time steelworkers earned fourteen cents an hour for a twelve-hour day, six or seven days a week. The company's profits had risen sixty percent, and the workers wanted their wages to rise accordingly. Frick saw things a little differently—as in a twenty-two-percent wage *cut*.

On June 29, 1892, one day before the contract expired, Frick locked the workers out of the Homestead Steel Works plant and built a high wooden fence around the perimeter, topped with barbed-wire and armed guard towers. The workers labeled it "Fort Frick" and went on strike the next day.

The union organized picket lines to ring the factory, with several hundred strikers occupying the space between the plant and the nearby Monongahela River. Hoping to crush the union once and for all, Frick hired three hundred Pinkerton strike-breakers and armed them with rifles. They were ordered to board barges and attack the picketers from the river.

In the early morning hours of July 6, the Pinkerton barges floated down the river and tried to land on the shore near the plant, but the strikers repulsed them. Soon bullets were flying from both sides, resulting in several deaths and injuries. A battle raged all day, until the outnumbered Pinkertons surrendered and left.

The exultant strikers' joy was short-lived. Pennsylvania Governor Robert Pattison, who had been elected with the help of the Carnegie Steel machine, sent in the state militia, which dispersed the picketers and let the plant open again with much cheaper, non-union "scabs."

Famous anarchist Emma Goldman and her lover, Alexander Berkman, were enraged by Frick's tactics and decided to murder the malicious steel-man. On July 23, 1892, armed with a pistol and knife, Berkman went to Frick's office in the Carnegie Building, which once stood at 428–438 Fifth Avenue, Pittsburgh (GPS 40.43969, -79.99763). Bursting through the door, Berkman fired twice at the tycoon, hitting him in the neck. A Frick aide grappled with Berkman, who still managed to stab Frick seven times, though none was deadly. Police carted Berkman off to jail, and Frick was back to work in a week.

Even though they had nothing to do with the attack, the steelworkers were hurt by the bad publicity, and eventually were forced to accept reduced-wage contracts as union membership plummeted. Frick won.

"Clayton," the 23-room mansion of steel magnate Henry Clay Frick

Unrepentant and unapologetic for the rest of his life, Frick died suddenly of a heart attack on December 2, 1919. When told of Frick's demise, would-be assassin Alexander Berkman, who had served his sentence for the assassination attempt and was now facing imminent deportation back to Russia, commented wryly that Frick had been "deported by God."

Frick is buried at Homewood Cemetery, 1599 South Dallas Avenue, Pittsburgh. His grave is in Section 14, Lot 66, or GPS 40.44288, -79.90840, on so-called "Millionaire's Hill" near Andrew Mellon's.

Frick's former twenty-three-room mansion, "Clayton," is open for tours at 133 South Homewood Avenue in Pittsburgh (GPS 40.44863, -79.90165). It's just a block north of the Frick Art and Historical Center, a museum open to the public.

DOG DAY AFTERNOON
Pittsburgh

The former Poplawski house is at 1016 Fairfield Street, or GPS 40.48476, -79.93954. This is private property.

One of the most dangerous situations a cop faces is a domestic dispute. They can turn ugly fast.

On April 4, 2009, Mary Poplawski called 911 and asked for police to remove her son, Richard, from the home for being verbally abusive as they argued over their dog's urinating on the floor.

When Officers Paul Sciullo and Stephen Mayhle arrived, Mary opened the door. What she didn't know was that Richard was standing behind her with a rifle aimed at the policemen. Before the startled cops could respond, Richard opened fire, killing both instantly. As a third officer, Eric Kelly, came up the walkway, Poplawski killed him, too.

A four-hour siege soon began. An army of cops exchanged more than six hundred rounds with Poplawski, who finally surrendered when he was wounded. Two other cops were also injured but survived. It was the first time in eighteen years that any Pittsburgh policemen had died on duty.

Poplawski received the death penalty.

Officer Sciullo is buried at St. Mary's Roman Catholic Cemetery, Penn Avenue and 45th Street in Pittsburgh. Mayhle is buried at Oakland Cemetery, Oakland Avenue and Rose Street in Indiana, Pennsylvania. Kelly is buried at Allegheny Cemetery, 4734 Butler Street in Pittsburgh. His grave is in Section 63, Lot 33-A, Grave 3.

MURDERED ATHEIST'S CHILDHOOD HOME
Pittsburgh

The former Mays home is at 1540 Beechview Avenue, or GPS 40.44109, -79.91695. This is private property.

Even as a child in Pittsburgh, Madalyn (Mays) Murray O'Hair was a pistol. After reading the entire Bible at age nine, she decided it was a crock and told her parents so.

To prove her point Madalyn went outside in a raging thunderstorm and yelled at the sky, defying God to strike her dead. When she survived she told her parents the test proved her right.

When she grew up and moved away from this childhood home, she led the charge to ban prayer in public schools and founded the American Atheists organization in Austin, Texas, earning her the sobriquet, "The Most Hated Woman in America."

On August 27, 1995, Madalyn, her son Jon Garth Murray, and granddaughter Robin, disappeared from their Austin home, leaving a terse note at their American Atheists headquarters. Many speculated the three had stolen the foundation's money and fled.

But six years later a federal investigation focused on David Roland Waters, an ex-con and former office manager of American Atheists who had embezzled $54,000 during O'Hair's tenure and who fantasized about murdering Madalyn in grisly ways. In a plea deal Waters finally admitted killing the three—plus a cohort—and led cops to the shallow grave on a Texas Hill Country ranch where he'd buried their remains (identifiable only through DNA, dental records and O'Hair's prosthetic hip).

Waters told investigators he'd extorted $500,000 in gold coins by kidnapping the O'Hairs. He and his girlfriend spent $80,000, but the rest (ironically) was stolen from a storage locker by burglars. Waters was convicted of extortion and money laundering—not kidnapping and murder—and imprisoned for life. He died in a North Carolina federal prison of lung cancer in 2003.

Slain atheist Madalyn Murray O'Hair lived here as a child.

Madalyn's remains were exhumed and given to her only remaining son, William—the same son at the center of her landmark school-prayer controversy. Per his mother's known wishes, he buried his family secretly to prevent prayers being said over them. Oddly, William, long-estranged from his mother, had become a born-again Christian and Baptist minister.

For more details, see *The Crime Buff's Guide to Outlaw Texas* (Globe Pequot Press, 2011).

THE REAL MRS. SOFFEL
Pittsburgh

The former Allegheny County Jail still stands at 440 Ross Street, or GPS 40.43861, -79.99580. It's now the Juvenile and Family Common Pleas Court.

Brothers Ed and Jack Biddle already had twenty-six robberies to their names when they held up a grocery store on April 12, 1901, and killed the store owner. Afterwards, they holed up in a nearby building, but police stormed the place. A cop was killed in the ensuing shootout, but the Biddles were captured. Eventually they were sentenced to hang and sent to the Allegheny Jail to await execution.

Kate Soffel, the warden's wife, spent her days reading the Bible to the prisoners, including the Biddles. Ed Biddle feigned interest and soon began to romance her with poetry and kind words, something she never got from her stuffy husband. Falling for Ed's charms Kate agreed to furnish the brothers with saws and guns to help them escape.

On January 30, 1902, Ed told a guard that Jack was sick and needed a doctor. When the guard opened the cell to see for himself, the Biddles beat him senseless and ran out to the street. Abandoning her husband and four children, Kate ran off with them. Stealing a sleigh and horses to navigate the winter snow, the trio headed north.

The cuckolded warden's posse caught up with them near Prospect, and a gun battle raged. The Biddles were mortally wounded, and Kate was also shot but not seriously. The criminals died the next day and were buried at Calvary Cemetery, 718 Hazelwood Avenue in Pittsburgh. Their mutual grave is halfway down the hill in Section 1, or GPS 40.41482, -79.93185. Also buried in the same cemetery is their policeman victim, Patrick Fitzgerald, in Section H, Lot 278, or GPS 40.41762, -79.93350.

Kate recovered and served two years at Western Penitentiary. Upon her release she tried to turn her notoriety into a vaudeville show, but it was closed down by the authorities before the first performance. She changed her name and became a seamstress, dying alone and forgotten on August 30, 1909. She is buried in an unmarked grave at Smithfield East End Cemetery, 1634 South Dallas Avenue in Pittsburgh.

The warden's wife, Mrs. Kate Soffel, facilitated a jailbreak from the Allegheny County Jail.

A 1984 movie, *Mrs. Soffel,* starring Diane Keaton and Mel Gibson, was filmed at the actual jail and renewed interest in her story. The filmmakers paid for the Biddles' grave-marker.

GROUNDHOG SKULLDUGGERY
Punxsutawney
Gobbler's Knob is in a rural setting off Woodland Avenue two miles east of town, at GPS 40.9302165, -78.9577237.

Easily Pennsylvania's most famous non-human citizen is Punxsutawney Phil, the groundhog who forecasts the length of winter every Groundhog Day. And when you're famous, trouble finds you.

You already know the legend: If Phil emerges from his winter hibernation and sees his shadow, there will be six more weeks of winter; no shadow means an early spring.

Every Groundhog Day, Punxsutawney Phil takes a risk as he emerges from his lair to predict when winter will end. JOHNSON BLUE

In 2005, Bam Margera, an actor on the television show *Jackass*, planned to kidnap Phil from his burrow before the big day. But word got out about the scheme, and as Margera and his cohorts stood before Phil's stump, they were surrounded by armed Pennsylvania state troopers, National Guardsmen, and "a few other large individuals." The kidnap plot was thwarted.

Years ago some marmot admirers in California were determined to start a West Coast branch of the Punxsutawney Groundhog Club. They requested a live groundhog for their festivities, but their Punxsutawney brethren sent them two. Tragically the State of California's very fussy Agriculture Department seized the groundhogs and executed them without a trial. The Punxsutawney club still refers to the bloodbath as "The Great California Groundhog Massacre."

A groundhog's life span is normally only about eight years, but Punxsutawney Phil has been around for decades. How's that possible? Well, legend says Phil gets a sip of a magical punch every summer, giving him seven more years of life each time.

So during Prohibition, Phil's handlers claim he made an unusual demand: He should be allowed to drink an alcoholic beverage or he would predict sixty more *years*—not weeks—of winter. The little drunkard must have gotten his wish.

MURDER AMONG THE AMISH
Rockdale Township

The former Gingerich home a half mile east of the intersection of Sturgis and Frisbeetown Roads, or GPS 41.84287, -79.93065. This is private property.

The Amish are among the most gentle, law-abiding people in America. But Ed Gingerich was not typical of the Order. He was lazy and bitter and chafed under the religion's strict rules.

Envying the pick-up trucks and telephones of his "English" friends, he saw no reason why he shouldn't have them. He also felt he had been pressured by Amish custom into marrying his wife, Katie, and resented her for it, virtually ignoring her and their children most of the time. After the birth of their third child, he refused to sleep with her and spent time with a married "English" woman who drove him around in her distinctly non-Amish bright red Jeep. When Katie confronted him about this, he would either hit her or storm away in a rage.

One day in 1992, Ed became dizzy and delusional after working in his machine shop with a potent solvent. When he started spitting at the ceiling and howling like a dog, Katie abandoned the homeopathic Amish remedies she had been using and admitted him to a mental hospital, where he stayed for two weeks.

Released with medication he was fine for a while, but the psychosis soon returned. He began screaming that his hair was on fire and that voices were telling him to kill Katie. He was admitted again and released ten days later. For several months, his demons were controlled . . . until March 18, 1993.

On that day the foreman of the Gingerich sawmill was getting married, and everyone in Brown Hill was invited. But Katie, afraid of how Ed might behave, kept the news from him. When Ed over-heard others talking about it, he declared he would attend. Katie told him he needed to rest instead, and he called her "the devil." After a short nap, he came into the kitchen, where Katie was wash-ing dishes, and their young children were playing on the floor, and again announced he was going to the wedding. Katie told him no and turned back to her task.

Enraged, Ed punched her in the face, sending her sprawling. She told their five-year-old son to summon Ed's brother, Danny, who lived nearby. As he obeyed, the younger children, ages four and three, sat rooted to the floor in fear.

Danny raced to the house and found Ed straddling Katie and beating her furiously. Danny tried to pull him away from her, but Ed fought him off. Before the startled eyes of the children and his brother, Ed stomped on Katie's head, splashing blood everywhere. Danny ran for help, and, finding a phone at an "English" farm down the street, called 911. But the EMTs wouldn't arrive in time.

Ed crushed his wife's skull with a final stomp of his heavy boot. He then ripped her clothing off and sliced open her abdomen, removing all her organs and laying them next to her body. Stabbing the knife into the gory pile, he informed his kids that he was taking them to stay at his parents' house across the street, and then would return to burn their house to the ground.

Paramedics were stunned by the carnage. State troopers carted Ed away as he answered their questions with bizarre and unintel-ligible ramblings.

Diagnosed as paranoid schizophrenic, Ed was convicted of involuntary manslaughter while mentally ill. He was sentenced to a short prison term and was freed one day after the fifth anniversary of Katie's death.

Katie was buried in the Grabhof Amish Cemetery, a half-mile northwest of the Gingerich house at GPS 41.85028, -79.93336. The cemetery is on the left side of a dirt road among a lot of brush and trees.

When Ed returned to the settlement, he was "shunned" and subsequently moved in with friends. He hanged himself in 2011 and is also buried in the Grabhof Amish Cemetery.

THE TWO WIVES OF TIM BOCZKOWSKI
Ross Township

The former Boczkowski home is at 306 Noring Court, or GPS 40.53936, -80.00558.

When both your marriage and your business are failing, what's a man to do? Tim Boczkowski's answer was to insure his wife for big bucks and kill her to collect it. He liked that idea so well he did it twice.

Married to Mary Elaine and living in North Carolina, Tim struggled to keep his ice cream stand afloat. When bankruptcy seemed certain, on November 4, 1990, he drowned Elaine in the bathtub at their apartment. Although suspicious, the coroner declared the death "undetermined," and Tim walked away with the insurance money and the couple's three young children. They returned to his hometown near Pittsburgh.

Within weeks he was dating a new woman, Maryann Fullerton. Around the same time he had his dead wife exhumed from North Carolina and re-buried nearby at St. Stanislaus Cemetery, 700 Soose Road in Millvale. The grave is in Section 5, under a large three-sided statue of the Holy Family at GPS 40.50766, -79.96408.

Two years later Tim and Maryann married. She loved Tim's kids, and they loved her. They even called her "Mom." But with Tim as their dad, they wouldn't get used to having a mother for long.

On November 7, 1994, showing an appalling lack of creativity, Tim drowned Maryann, too—this time in the hot tub on their back porch. But Tim had gone to the well once too often. As Pittsburgh police learned what happened to wife number one, the coroner was finding signs of strangulation on wife number two.

Tim was arrested. Tried first in North Carolina, he was convicted and sentenced to life. After his Pennsylvania conviction, he received a death sentence, which was overturned; he is now serving a life term.

Maryann was buried in St. Anthony's Cemetery (adjacent to St. Stanislaus), 700 Soose Road, in Section F at GPS 40.50499, -79.96667.

NUN'S MURDER GOES COLD
Sharpsburg

St. Mary's Cemetery is at 1019 Sharps Hill Road. The grave is at Section E, Block 1, Lot 9, or GPS 40.506734, -79.936171.

In November 1969, Pennsylvania-born Sister Catherine Ann Cesnik (b. 1942) was returning to her Baltimore apartment after a shopping trip when she disappeared. Two months later the well-liked, twenty-six-year-old teacher's badly decomposed and vermin-eaten body was found in a snowy, vacant field. Although police couldn't tell much from her remains, the back of her skull bore a hole the size of a quarter.

Sister Cathy's Carriage House Apartments are at 131 North Bend Road in Baltimore, or GPS 39.282385, -76.705337. Sister Cathy had been granted "exclaustration"—permission from the Church to live outside the convent under relaxed vows.

Cops focused on the Catholic school where Sister Cathy had recently taught, Archbishop Keough High School for Girls (now Seton Keough High School), 1201 Caton Avenue in Baltimore (GPS 39.269167, -76.666111). Detectives were disturbed by rumors of rampant sexual misbehavior at the school and theorized that Sister Cathy might have planned to blow the whistle.

Investigators grilled Sister Cathy's acquaintances, including a Jesuit priest with whom she had a romantic relationship, and an allegedly abusive priest at the school.

But the trail went cold, and Sister Cathy's killer has never been identified, although cold-case detectives recently took a new look at the killing without success.

Raised in a small town in rural Pennsylvania, she was buried near her childhood home.

THE MYSTERIOUS DEATH OF BETSY AARDSMA
State College
Pattee Library is on Curtin Road on the campus of Penn State University at GPS 40.79799, -77.86642. The BA stacks are one floor down from the library lobby, or GPS 40.79846, -77.86589.

A dedicated scholar, Betsy Aardsma was a pretty, twenty-two-year-old Penn State graduate student who had decided to spend the Thanksgiving break on campus instead of going home to Michigan. She was working on a special project for her English professor and wanted to get some work done in the holiday quiet. In fact, when she met with the professor on November 28, 1969, he expressed interest in a book she had previously recommended, so she told him she would fetch it from the library for him. Later she met a friend in the library and told her about her impending trip to the BA stacks, a confined area under the main floor of the building.

Taking a claustrophobic stairway down to the stacks, Aardsma poked around the jungle of shelves looking for the book. Her friend came down to visit her twice—once to borrow a pen and the other to return it. Betsy seemed fine, and the friend noticed nothing unusual.

But shortly after the friend left for the second time, a loud crash reverberated through the stacks, causing two students nearby to investigate. A young man rushed up to them, shouting, "Somebody better help that girl!" He led them to Betsy, who lay on the floor, books scattered all around her. He then ran up the steps and out of the library.

Betsy, who was wearing a bright red dress, appeared to have fainted. But it was only at the hospital that doctors found that

211

the hue of her dress had disguised a single knife wound that had pierced her heart. She was dead.

Although the witnesses in the stacks were later hypnotized and provided a police sketch-artist with a description of the mysterious stranger's face, no one recognized him or came forward with information. Betsy's murder is still unsolved and remains one of the enduring mysteries of the college town.

But the story doesn't end there. On December 3, 1994, shortly after the twenty-fifth anniversary of Betsy's slaying, a burning candle and scattered news-clippings about the crime were found in the stacks on the spot where Betsy fell. On the floor, written in red, were the words, "RIP Betsy Ruth Aardsma, July 11, 1947–November 28, 1969. P.S. I'm back."

The BA stacks where Betsy Aardsma was murdered

PENN STATE PEDOPHILE SCANDAL
State College

The Second Mile is at 1402 South Atherton Street, or GPS 40.78474, -77.84133.

On November 5, 2011, Jerry Sandusky, a former assistant to college football coaching legend Joe Paterno, was arrested for sexually molesting at least ten boys who lived at The Second Mile, a group home he founded in 1977. For years, enticing them with trips to the stadium and the thrall of big-time college football, he lured them into the locker room, where he was seen by different Penn State employees engaging in sexual behavior with them in the showers. The university's administration quelled the situation in-house by merely taking away Sandusky's keys to the locker room. They never reported the incidents to the authorities.

A previous investigation in 1998, started by complaints by some victims' mothers, was dropped by District Attorney Ray Gricar (who, strangely, inexplicably disappeared in 2005 while on an antiquing trip and was never seen again). But in 2009 the Pennsylvania Attorney General re-opened the case when more allegations surfaced. The scandal broke wide open with Sandusky's surprise arrest, and the resulting uproar resulted in the firing of Paterno, athletic director Tim Curley, and university president Graham Spanier.

On June 22, 2012, Sandusky was convicted of forty-five counts, including indecent assault and endangering the welfare of children. He will spend the rest of his life in prison.

"LET'S ROLL"
Stoystown/Shanksville area

The Flight 93 Memorial entrance is at 6424 Lincoln Highway, at GPS 40.081772, -78.885920. The memorial is open from 10 a.m. to 7 p.m. daily. Admission is free.

On that dark day, September 11, 2001, Americans were especially touched by the bravery and sacrifice of the hijacked passengers on United Flight 93.

Flight 93 departed shortly after 8 a.m. from Newark, New Jersey, bound for San Francisco. The Boeing 757 carrying forty-four people was delayed on the runway for several minutes. Less than an hour into the flight, somewhere near Cleveland, Islamic terrorists, who had previously been quiet passengers, sprang into action. Brandishing box cutters, they announced they were taking over the plane, and Flight 93 abruptly reversed course. Stunned, the passengers called their loved ones by cell phone and learned that other hijacked planes had been flown into the World Trade Center and the Pentagon. Realizing they faced a similar fate, the passengers planned a counterattack. Under Todd Beamer's cry of "Let's roll!" a group of them stormed the cockpit and fought with the hijackers, who sent the plane into a dive, crashing it into an empty field near Stoystown. Everyone on board—forty passengers and crew, plus four hijackers—was killed.

A spontaneous memorial that went up soon after the crash has been replaced by a much larger, permanent one being built by the National Park Service. A huge white wall at the end of a long walkway is engraved with the names of the passengers who died that day. The actual crash site (GPS 40.050270, -78.902317) can be visited only by victims' family members, but can be seen from a vantage point nearby.

The memorial was dedicated on September 10, 2011, the day before the tenth anniversary of the crash of Flight 93.

The story is retold in the 2006 TV movie, *Flight 93*.

THE "TOTAL RECALL" MURDER
Wilkinsburg

The former Mudd home is at 1515 Marlboro Avenue, or GPS 40.43882, -79.87032. This is private property.

This case reads like a Hollywood script—a battered wife, an illicit affair, shots ringing out in the dark, a dead husband lying at the bottom of the stairs, and a child's repressed memory of the murder coming back to him as an adult. But for John Mudd, it was all too real.

John and Arlene Mudd's marriage was not made in Heaven. Infidelity, screaming matches, and physical abuse were common in their home. In 1975, Arlene found a sympathetic ear and a warm bed with Steve Slutzker, her neighbor across the street at 1516 Marlboro Avenue (GPS 40.43892, -79.87033).

When John discovered the affair, a tug-of-war ensued between the two men over their rather frumpy prize. The pawn in all this drama was five-year-old John Mudd Jr., who had already experienced more parental strife than any child should. Guns were pulled and threats were made, and still Arlene couldn't decide between her two suitors. Slutzker decided to save her the trouble.

On December 28, 1975, Arlene, John, and John Jr. were snuggled together in a rare moment of domestic harmony in their living room, watching television, when the power suddenly went out. John went to check the basement fuse-box, but halfway down the stairs he was hit by a barrage of gunfire. Tumbling to the basement floor, he died instantly.

Police suspected Slutzker was the killer but had no proof. For fifteen years the crime went unsolved. John Jr. grew up with relatives and was virtually abandoned by his mother, who managed to marry and divorce twice more during that period, neither time to Slutzker.

On November 23, 1990, John Jr. suddenly had a flashback to the night of the murder. In his mind's eye, he could see his father's body at the bottom of the stairs and Steve Slutzker emerging from the basement and talking to his mother. The image reduced him to tears as his friends and family called police.

Slutzker went to trial where experts battled over whether the recovered vision was real. Although not fully convinced of Junior's story, the jury felt there was enough other evidence to convict Slutzker, and he was sentenced to life in prison. Arlene was never tried.

ACKNOWLEDGMENTS

As always, many people helped make this book possible.

Karen's dad entertained her and kept her awake on their travels to the far corners of their home state. Her son Aaron's eagle eye spotted many a hidden gravestone. And cousin Penny Beitman knew Harrisburg and Carlisle like the back of her hand.

Once again, Ron's wife Mary played her usual crucial role as an invaluable sounding board, adviser, and copy editor.

Thanks also go to Ann Rushow for her support and to her husband, George Rushow, whose knowledge of the coal regions was positively encyclopedic. He led us through long-forgotten mining patches and lonely graveyards.

We also wish to thank the staff of all those cemeteries we called or visited, who looked up and plotted out on maps the graves for which we searched. Standing out among these was Diane Amole of Morris Cemetery, who dug through dusty old volumes of records from the 1800s to find the Longabaugh graves, and Kenneth Turpin, Paul Sookiasion, and Mary Malinowski, who literally escorted Karen to the gravesites she was seeking. Thanks also to Joseph Cammie and Mary Briggeman, who were instrumental in our discovery of the final resting place of the Old West's last outlaw and native Pennsylvanian, Wild Bill Carlisle—something no western historian has ever been able to do.

Thank you to the many strangers who gave directions, supplied information, and told colorful tales of their local crimes and legends. And to the staff of the Exeter Diner, who kept Karen fed, hydrated, and free "WiFi-ed" through all the stages of her research and writing. Their kind attention and moral support kept her going.

Above all, we owe our deepest gratitude to all the crime buffs, armchair historians, and day-trippers who love reading these stories as much as we love telling them. Now go out and chase some of these ghosts.

—Ron Franscell & Karen B. Valentine

INDEX

ABOUT THE AUTHORS

Ron Franscell is a best-selling author and journalist whose atmospheric true crime/memoir *The Darkest Night* was hailed as a direct descendant of Truman Capote's *In Cold Blood* and established him as one of the most provocative new voices in narrative nonfiction. His work  has appeared in the *Washington Post*, *Chicago Sun-Times*, *San Francisco Chronicle*, *Denver Post*, *San Jose Mercury-News*, *St. Louis Post-Dispatch*, and *Milwaukee Journal-Sentinel*. *The Crime Buff's Guide to Outlaw Pennsylvania* is his fifth book for Globe Pequot Press. Ron grew up in Wyoming and now lives in Texas.

Karen B. Valentine, a lifelong native of the Keystone State, has been a crime buff since she first learned to read. She lives in Eastern Pennsylvania with her grown son, Aaron, and her Shih-Tzu, Scrappy. This is her first book.